# MARKETS 101

# MARKETS 101

Kevin Koy

MLS Publishing
a division of
Market Logic Group, Ltd.

Printed in the United States of America
First Edition
Book Design by Paul Higdon

ISBN 0-941275-01-9

## Acknowledgments

I would like to express my appreciation to many people who either directly or indirectly helped me with this book, including: Nina Brannigan, Dan Gramza, David Hale, Steven Hawkins, Peter Hicks, Elle Jackson, Maureen H. Koy, Steven Kotz, George Kratzner, Connie Lee, Steven Mardiks, Brendan Moynihan, Lennart Palme, Chuck Pettet, Steven Pingry, John Powers, Roy Postel, Linda Racaniello, Kevin Riley, Jock Shoemaker, Randy Shell, Thomas and Charlotte Smith.

**Special thanks to the following companies who provided data or graphics used in the production of "Markets 101".**

**Technical Trading Strategies, Inc.**
4877 S. Everett Street
Littleton, CO 80123
(303) 972-1433

**Tick Data, Inc.**
720 Kipling Street
Suite 115
Lakewood, CO 80215
(303) 232-3701

**FutureSource** (division of)
Commodity Communications Corporations
250 Wacker Drive
Suite 1150
Chicago, IL 60606
(312) 977-9067
(800) 992-9277

**Knight-Ridder Tradecenter**
25 Hudson Street
New York, NY 10013
(212) 226-4700

**Commodity Quote Graphics**
P.O. Box 758
Glenwood Springs, CO 81602
(303) 945-8686
(800) 525-7082

# TABLE OF CONTENTS

AUTHOR'S FOREWORD . . . . . . . . . . . . . . . . . . . .xi
INTRODUCTION . . . . . . . . . . . . . . . . . . . . . . . . .xv

**SECTION ONE: How Active Markets Function**

CHAPTER 1.   COMMON SENSE AND
MARKETS . . . . . . . . . . . . . . . . . . .3
CHAPTER 2.   PRINCIPLES OF TRADE
FACILITATION . . . . . . . . . . . . . . .7
CHAPTER 3.   PRINCIPLES OF MARKET
LOGIC . . . . . . . . . . . . . . . . . . . . . .13
CHAPTER 4.   PRINCIPLES OF AUCTIONS  23
CHAPTER 5.   OBSERVATIONS DEFINED
AND CHARACTERIZED:
MARKET BACKGROUND AND
DEFINITIONS . . . . . . . . . . . . . . .29

**SECTION TWO: Organizing Markets to Read
Market-Generated Information**

CHAPTER 6.   THE IMPORTANCE OF
ASSESSING VALUE . . . . . . . . .43
CHAPTER 7.   GROUPING PARTICIPANTS
ACCORDING TO TIMEFRAME
. . . . . . . . . . . . . . . . . . . . . . . . . . .47
CHAPTER 8.   THE BELL CURVE: GIVING
STRUCTURE AND MEANING
TO THE MARKET . . . . . . . . . . .53
CHAPTER 9.   DEFINED OPPORTUNITIES
AND THE TYPES OF
RESPONSE . . . . . . . . . . . . . . . . .63
CHAPTER 10.   ORGANIZING DATA TO
DETERMINE THE TREND . . .71
CHAPTER 11.   DAY STRUCTURES . . . . . . . . .79
CHAPTER 12.   HOW THE DIFFERENT DAY
STRUCTURES INTERACT . . .95

**SECTION THREE: Decision-Making with Market-Generated Information: Interpreting Reference Points**

CHAPTER 13.    AN OVERVIEW OF DECISION-MAKING IN THE FINANCIAL MARKETS ..................111

CHAPTER 14.    MARKET ACTIVITY NUANCES AND SUBTLETIES .........115

CHAPTER 15.    TECHNICAL ANALYSIS AND MARKET LOGIC ...........123

CHAPTER 16.    MICRO ANALYSIS: DEUTSCHE MARK ....................157

CHAPTER 17.    EVOLUTION OF THE LEARNING PROCESS......269

# AUTHOR'S FOREWORD

Long-term investors seek to beat the equity, fixed income, currency and agricultural commodity markets with a decision-making process which relies on some mixture of research, intuition and luck. Specialists, floor traders, market-makers, arbitrageurs and other professionals who compete in the stock, futures and options markets using a shorter time horizon than the long-term investor also wish to do better than the market. These two groups compete with one another and other nonprofessionals in an environment where prices are supposedly discovered in a statistically random fashion. But the very existence of the Warren Buffetts, John Templetons, etc., on the one hand, and the many prosperous short time horizon market-makers, folks who collectively make up the world financial market's floor community, on the other, troubles the random walk theorist. The fact that these two groups tend to consistently beat the market averages informs us that random walk and efficient market theories just don't represent the reality of the financial world. Being a pragmatic individual, I was troubled by this. Back when I studied economics in the theoretical world of higher education, and later as co-founder and editor of *Intermarket* I repeatedly came face to face with a paradox: on the one hand, I was told the financial market was a random walk, unbeatable over any large sample size. On the other hand, I came face to face with the non-random results. Common sense told me that certain individuals who consistently — whether measured yearly, quarterly, or in the case of floor participants even monthly or weekly — take profits from the market over a large sample size of trades must have both information and a logical market approach based on a well-grounded understanding of reality. Simply stated, they must have an edge. They must be doing something that the others aren't.

But if I accepted the notion that financial markets were somehow different from the rest of the world's everyday, unorganized, non-exchange-traded markets, then what could these informational or decision-making parameters possibly be? It's as if wealth were being allocated not randomly, but only to those financial market competitors with the very shortest and the very longest time horizons and away from those competitors in the middle.

Could it be that the decision-making process of the avowed Graham and Dodd group of Buffett, Templeton, Ruane, et al was in some way similar to that of the successful floor participants in the world's major exchanges? I set out to answer this question.

I interviewed numerous very successful traders, and exchanged ideas with all of them.

Not that the concept of randomness was some arcane theoretical proposition that I hoped to slay. Rather, random walk is applied on a daily basis throughout the financial world and can be blamed for many evils; it lies at the base of the fear and emotionalism that dominate people who tend not to do well in the financial markets. The fear that price discovery occurs randomly pervades most participants, and if they do not overcome this disinformation through observation-based experience, they are destined to fail.

It was with this knowledge that I undertook

what may be the most compelling adventure of my life — setting up what I believe to be the first school that teaches a consistent and logical trading decision-making process. I, along with floor trader Pete Steidlmayer, founded the Market Logic School in 1986. Our idea was to offer an educational curriculum offering decision-making insights that would otherwise take the individual years to discover. It is my hope that through the work for which the Market Logic School has become noted, the random walk theory will soon become an anachronism, even in the academic community. It clearly is obsolete as a description of market reality, but it will take time for the financial scholars to accept this and adjust.

# Introduction

**F**ew enter into the frenzied financial markets expecting to fail. However, it is a reality that the majority who do try their hand, particularly in leveraged financial products, stagger out of the experience as financial losers. Why is this so? Certainly the lack of a solid market approach, inadequate market knowledge, and the propensity toward emotional decision-making contribute to their defeat. But perhaps failure over the long term lies in a more fundamental failing, one which towers over the realms of market analysis or a human being's rash behavior. Too many traders ignore the fact that participation in the financial markets is first and foremost a business endeavor. Professionals in areas outside the financial markets begin with a methodical, structured format that clearly emphasizes sound business principles. All entrepreneurs must apply these same business principles if their dream product or service can ever become a market reality. Yet traders and investors frequently stray from what is a traditionally successful mode of operation.

A successful approach to financial markets, it would seem, would spring forth from some simple propositions made by successful entrepreneurs remarking on what made them successful in their specific product or service niche. They know that their particular market is neither mystical nor foreboding, but in fact is understandable and approachable. More fundamentally, they truly appreciate the pervasiveness of free markets and

they respect the market's role as a benevolent
final arbiter of economic endeavor. They have discovered through experience certain insights and
tools which allow them to understand their particular market's reality. From there they can make
logical deductions, decide a reasonable course of
action and strive to make rational, unemotional
decisions based on business principles.

To a limited extent some financial market participants follow a part of this approach. A trader's
understanding and comfort in a given unorganized market is usually not developed through a
formal educational curriculum. Rather, it is
arrived at slowly through experience and at times
unconsciously through trial and error. The entry
level participant is rarely aware his comfort level
in a market he does understand is transferable to
the financial market. In time he learns that by
operating based on the same principles he applies
in other markets, he can successfully compete in
the financial marketplace.

While the majority of this book's readers are
interested only in the financial markets, the
book's title does not specify only them. This has
been done to underscore a paradox which has created confusion among market participants:
organized, exchange-traded financial markets
have been intellectually isolated, treated as if they
were entirely different in both spirit and makeup
from other "understandable" markets. Financial
markets have not been seen as one subgroup of
the arena of marketplaces, and as such, a subgroup where the same principles which hold true
in the broader arenas apply. Instead, because
they deal in the creation and destruction of
wealth, a generally emotion-laden topic, they are
put on a higher plane, and are considered mystical, foreboding and complex.

As such, the financial markets have become misunderstood not only by the so-called man on the street, but also by the majority of market participants. Financial markets are in fact misunderstood because most people — functional in everyday understandable situations — assume their decision-making process is not in any way applicable to formulating a buy-sell decision-making strategy in the financial markets. And so they remain mystified, intimidated and in awe of financial markets.

# SECTION ONE:

# How Active Markets Function

This section will discuss the purpose of every market, and the market's components which make it function. It will describe how, in an active phase, these components interact and thereby allow the market to carry out its purpose. The reader will see how, as in any business endeavor, the task of the financial market participant is to concentrate not on what the future may bring, but on what the market's present condition indicates.

# Chapter 1

# Common Sense and Markets

Although it is not general knowledge, it is a fact that the successful market participant — whether the long timeframe Graham and Dodd "value" investor or the short timeframe floor local — concentrates on current information rather than on trying to predict how the future will unfold. Focusing on the present allows the trader to employ a decision-making and management approach similar to that of other professionals. For example, it is a rare medical doctor who will give a straight answer to the question, "When will I be well enough to leave this hospital?" The M.D. does not concentrate on predicting a future fraught with uncertainties. He knows that the possible outcomes are compounded by the many variables influencing the patient's situation — his current symptoms, his condition and overall strength, the possible causes of the ailment, the possible remedies, what, if any, allergic reaction the patient may have to medication, etc. The doctor, like the lawyer, accountant, or other professional offering service in a complex and uncertain world, knows that he can be wrong when he attempts to predict or forecast future outcomes.

The professional knows that he need not expose himself to the possibility of being wrong about future outcomes so long as he adjusts as he receives new information. Professionals are trained to investigate, to seek highly specialized

cues or messages which give meaning to or insight
into the current situation. These cues often allow
them to intuit, extrapolate or infer conclusions or
possible scenarios under various conditions.
Hence a professional's conclusions are not based
on forecasting the future, but on what the current
cues and messages mean to the task at hand,
based on deductive logic given the professional's
experience.

To bring this point home, consider the operational procedures of the above-mentioned M.D. He
monitors his patient's variables (breathing, pulse
rate, body temperature, brain waves, etc.) knowing two important truisms which are implicit in
his experience and his professional approach.
First, the doctor knows that by observing these
variables, he will most likely extract some mes-
sage or cue from them. From this, he hopes to
interpret the cause of the patient's illness. At
worst, he will rule out certain possible causes.
Second, the doctor knows that, in the trader's ver-
nacular, the trend is his friend. In other words, as
he treats the patient, continuing to monitor the
patient's variables, he gains confidence in his
course of action if the patient gets better and the
recovery appears to be unfolding as he expects. If,
after receiving treatment, the patient does not
improve or gets worse, the doctor will hope to
receive other cues as to how to adjust, and will
suggest a new remedy.

The key to the success of the professional, then,
lies in

    a)  executing an action plan formulated
        from logical, experience-based deduc-
        tive reasoning based on information
        describing current conditions;
    b)  maintaining the managerial flexibility

required to adjust as conditions change.

In other words, the professional arrives at conclusions or expectations through continual and intensive review of new information as it unfolds. He adjusts based on changes which may be occurring in the overall picture. This identical challenge faces the participant in any market, financial or otherwise.

The remainder of this book will identify those cues that the professional financial market participant needs to recognize as he builds the experience required to follow a consistent decision-making process. Several markets which most readers are probably familiar with will be referred to. Hopefully, this will provide a cross-referencing mechanism, making the concepts easier to grasp and demonstrating with practical examples that the principles of all markets are the same.

# Chapter 2

## Principles of Trade Facilitation

An investigation into how a given concept or tool can be practically applied or used — or how an organism functions — must begin by defining its purpose. Describing a flexible piece of sturdy sheet metal with a sharp, jagged edge and a handle attached does little to advance an amateur carpenter's working knowledge of how to accomplish his goals with it. Disclosing that the purpose of this implement is to saw or cut through relatively thin pieces of wood or pipe opens up many possibilities for use.

Gaining a working knowledge of markets and a logical methodology for prospering in the financial markets also requires a basic understanding of the purpose of the market. What then is its purpose? A common belief is that the purpose of the market is to balance supply and demand and to allocate scarce resources. Consider for a moment whether the market in fact does these things. Although the market is first and foremost a balancing mechanism, its balancing behavior is caused by (and hence reflects) the collective or net opinion of all currently active participants. Some obviously represent those parties in tune with the consumer or demand factors while others represent the suppliers. Many participants represent neither party, but seek to profit.

7

The question arises, is the market at any one time truly balanced? On any given day, the currently active participants' collective buy-sell activities cause a range of prices to be discovered. Current market behavior, then, is merely a reflection of the behavior of a group of "currently active" people. It is therefore illogical to assume that the market is efficient (i.e., that price reflects everyone's opinion) in the short run.

Perceptions of what is fair value, what is an attractive opportunity, and what one's needs are at a given price vary among people. Students of human nature agree that human perception is rarely an accurate reflection of reality. Manias, financial bubbles and panics are all outgrowths of collective or individual human conduct. Perception is rarely unanimous, or in balance, and the differing opinions of fair value mean that the market will not be in balance very often. From a practical standpoint, this means that the market's most recent price is always unfair and is advertising an opportunity for some group of buyers or sellers among the spectrum of traders.

Change affects people on a psychological level, their reaction again being affected by their particular situation. At certain times, the dominant group may be resistant to change, while at other times it may be anticipating, willing to accept and even welcome change. People do not react to change in the same ways, which is why markets, when experiencing change (i.e., a trend), tend to be very volatile. The greater the rate of change, the greater the degree of volatility. **In the final analysis, human behavior, which is dynamic, evolving and ever changing, creates market behavior. Markets are merely humans reacting or not reacting to information and opportunities.**

These thoughts are included to illustrate the inadequacy of the conventional supposition that the purpose of the marketplace is to balance supply and demand and allocate scarce resources. Since this is an impossible task, the supposition must be incorrect. We cannot conclude that in the short run markets do indeed balance supply and demand. They merely balance the market by making the situation fair between the most recently active buyers and sellers.

The methodological approach promulgated and practiced by the Market Logic School differs from current academic wisdom on markets, here, at the very outset.

**The purpose of any market is to facilitate trade, to transact or conduct an increased amount of business.**

The self-interest of participants dictates that this is so. If a market isn't fair for one side of the buyer/seller group, that side which considers itself unfairly disadvantaged by price will not trade, and the transactional volume will fall off. Thus, to facilitate trade, the market seeks to find an area where prices are perceived as fair for both buyer and seller.

The above statement of purpose defines a free market, one in which its participants are free to engage in buying or selling of the underlying entity being traded as their self-interest dictates. Such a marketplace exists solely to facilitate trade. This is its one and only purpose.

But while the market does not exist to allocate scarce resources and balance supply and demand, it does in the long run balance supply and demand and at any one moment does allocate (and continually reallocates) the scarce resources traded in a free market. To continue an earlier analogy, consider the confusion of the lay carpenter if he embraced the same logical fallacy that hinders the majority of market participants — mistaking the purpose for one result of the entity fulfilling its purpose. Suppose the carpenter were to mistake the saw's purpose — to slice thin wood — for an ancillary result of the saw's fulfilling its purpose — say, to create sawdust. He would find that his false conception of the saw's purpose would not help him see how the saw would make his job easier. It is imperative, therefore, not to be misled and mistakenly confuse the outward results of the marketplace — that price is rationing supply and demand — with its purpose, its **raison d'etre**.

Consider as an example of the implications of this concept the crude oil market during the 1970s. When prices were at $30/bbl., the market was allocating a scarce resource and balancing supply and demand, as it was at $10/bbl. But due to the self-interest of individual and corporate energy consumers, the market was not facilitating nearly the level of trade at $30/bbl., which is why the price eventually fell to $10/bbl. The point is that the market over the short run "allocates" and over the long run "balances" at any price. But it does not necessarily facilitate trade at any price. The process of allocating and balancing in the long run is a result of the market fulfilling its sole purpose — to facilitate trade.

Grasping the primary importance of a market's need to facilitate trade is the backbone of an understanding of an everyday market, because it indicates the ability of the market to continue directionally. In other words, the degree to which a market facilitates trade is important market-generated information which indicates the strength of a directional price movement. Oil prices during the 1970s rose to such levels that the multitude of conservation efforts soon dropped demand drastically. Anyone who observed that the local gas station was selling fewer gallons of gasoline per week at the relatively high prices knew the trend toward higher fuel costs was doomed.

Knowing the degree to which the market is facilitating trade, then, is one of the keys to understanding a market. Yet measuring this degree can often be difficult for the casual observer. There are several methods of measuring the degree to which a market facilitates trade. They include:

1) comparing total transactions occurring over different but equivalent units of time, such as two consecutive days.

2) comparing the high-low range of prices transacted over consistent time increments. The assumption is that the larger the range, the greater the participation and market acceptance. The smaller range shows a smaller degree of participation and probably the diminishing of satisfaction.

3) organizing transactional data via normal distribution. More information on this will be given later in this book.

After dwelling on the trade facilitation principle, it becomes obvious that all market participants understand that the purpose of an everyday market is to facilitate trade. Also obvious is that in the process of attempting to facilitate trade and either succeeding or failing to do so, the market generates valuable information for the participants. This is the single most important insight into the inner workings of everyday markets. This information flow provides a measure of results which illuminates for the discerning participant the current condition of the market. "Conditions" indicate whether the market can be expected to continue in its recent direction, or trend, or whether that trend is climaxing and thus may be changing direction.

In seeking to facilitate the greatest amount of trade, a market continually tests different price levels. Through this process — the ongoing probing back and forth between higher and lower price levels — the market again generates this same valuable information, both to those who are actively involved, and to those who are peripherally involved and merely observing. The information garnered from the market's rotation — its probing back and forth — relates to the direction in which price is moving over time.

# Chapter 3

# Principles of Market Logic

Proponents of Market Logic assert that the market's components interact in a logical fashion, and that current conditions indeed can be understood. This chapter will provide an understanding of the components the marketplace uses to facilitate trade, advertise opportunity, and otherwise generate information.

Every marketplace functions with five components: the product and the interests of the producer-participant, the need on the part of the consumer-participant, a centralized location or network providing communication, price, and time.

*The Product and the Interests of the Producer-Participant*

The product must satisfy a need, or else be packaged or marketed in such a way as to persuade the participants that it satisfies a need. The producer is a self-interested individual whose need is to remain in business and whose goal is to maximize profits. He wishes to facilitate trade in his product in order to determine the price at which profits are maximized.

*The Need on the Part of the Consumer-Participant*

Consumer-participants have their own individual purposes for using the market. These purposes are many and varied, and in all but the most organized markets they reflect the consumer's need for the product. The participant's goal is to fulfill his need as cost-effectively as possible and to determine the quantity of purchase needed to do so. Every product has a value in the mind of each consumer. In assessing the product's value, each consumer weighs the product's costs and benefits through time.

Significantly, the decision-making behavior of both consumer and producer is influenced by participant timeframes. Each active participant is restricted to some degree by the amount of time he has to make his transaction. Those who need to buy an item right away, for instance, have a short timeframe, while those who do not have a pressing need have the luxury of time and hence a long timeframe.

If it could be done, organizing a market's participants along a spectrum of timeframes from shortest timeframe to longest would provide invaluable information for those wishing to profit from a market. The behavior of shorter timeframe participants would be discounted somewhat, since they must transact soon anyway. But when the individuals who are known to be long timeframe participants entered the market, an opportunity to transact at those same prices would be apparent. This is because the observer, knowing that long timeframe participants do not need to act immediately, would deduce from the fact of their participation now that prices were sufficiently attractive to prompt them to enter the market.

However, accurately organizing all the market's participants along a timeframe spectrum according to either your own estimation or the participants' statements of their individual timeframes is difficult if not impossible. The reliability of data gathered would be suspect, given that a) the only means of objectively gaining such insight would be to question competing market participants, and b) we all continually shift our own timeframe depending on our circumstances at the moment. Even if possible, such information would reflect only current conditions, and thus become quickly outdated as conditions change. In other words, the timeframes change too fast for the trader to reasonably exploit his knowledge.

### A Centralized Location or Network

All markets have either centralized locations or a network offering communications among market participants. This is an integral component of the market because, whether it is centralized or dispersed, the market has hours of business. A business's closing time inserts a potential forcing point for decision-making. Thus, participants may act differently early or midway into a trading session than they will toward the close of trading. Other examples of market-imposed timeframes include the release of a report, contract expiration and a board of directors meeting (for a stock), etc.

### Price

Price, the market component most participants rely on when making trading decisions, is the amount of money given or set as consideration for the sale of a specified item. It is a variable and, as such, it fluctuates. Price facilitates trade by balancing the market, making the situation fair for both producer and consumer over the very short run.

The market, in facilitating trade, uses price to

promote activity. Price does this by advertising opportunity, moving up or down in order to make the market attractive for participants to enter. The market continually shifts or vacillates between price areas where buying (consuming) and selling (producing) are encouraged. In other words, price tests excess levels. However, the market has little or no trade activity when price moves either too high or too low. When this occurs, the market does not facilitate trade, forcing prices to change eventually.

To prevent price from moving too extensively in one direction, the marketplace has "hidden brakes," namely, the self-interest of the participants. If price becomes unfairly above or below value, one of the parties to the producer-consumer equation will not trade or will trade in decreasing volume. For example, as price moves up, the market advertises opportunity for producers, but may be in an area where the consumers will not buy, or will buy grudgingly and in smaller volume, thus forcing the producers to lower price over time.

The promotional ability of excess price and the hidden brakes inherent in every marketplace can be illustrated by a business custom existing in most Western cultures, the "post-holiday sale." During this period, most department stores substantially discount merchandise not sold at regular prices during the holiday season when the retailer has greatest inventory demand. Store management realizes that after the holiday season a shortage of buyers exists, and merchandise not sold at regular pre-holiday prices will not move quickly. The retailer's primary goal throughout the year is to be quickly rid of slow-moving inventory (which is costing interest, storage and insurance) while always increasing liquidity.

Hence, merchandise is repriced downward. Furthermore, merchandise will be sold only if repriced at enough of a discount to attract bargain hunters. Thus, every post-holiday sale is a market's use of a "purpose (low excess) price" designed to move old inventory not sold during the holiday season. The retailer is willing to promote his leftover inventory through an excess low price, since only the excess price reduction will accomplish the goal.

Shoppers perceive these new lower prices as bargains because for the months leading into the holidays, these same items cost much more. For example, a shirt which had sold for $50 in the previous nine months, offered after the holidays for $25, gets participants to react. They realize they're buying price below the value established over the prior months. Thus, shoppers have an association of price over time equaling value, not as an acknowledged and articulated principle, but rather as a perceived, almost unconscious insight. The hidden brake which prevents the shirt from selling for $10 is the self-interest of the retailer, who assumes that 50% off will be as much of a price excess as he needs to fulfill his goal in the time allocated.

While a low price excess attracts consumers, a high price excess similarly attracts producers. An example of the latter can be seen in the prices hotels can charge when demand for hotel rooms is created.

The managements of seasonal motels located in resort areas expect a strong demand, and thus charge the highest prices only during the seasonal periods. Suppose that a major amusement theme park opens some miles away from hotel facilities, creating vast demand for nearby hotel space. A lone hotel next to the park is now able to charge

twice what the faraway accommodations charge
during the off-season, yet still remains fully
booked. This high or excess price charged by the
lone hotel is providing information to competitors.
This information will inevitably promote activity in
land values around the resort park, since vendors
of resort-related services envision substantial
profits, profits the lone hotel is making. Thus,
high prices attract more (producers) sellers, who
buy up land (at higher values) and build hotels.
The so-called hidden brakes — the self-interest of
the participants assuming a fixed demand — will
insure that prices will fall and the excess price
charged by the lone hotel will soon be lowered to
maximize profitability.

Thus, one of the most important insights that
the marketplace will give to both producer and
consumer is that activity is being shut off at a
certain price. This is a signal that price is not
facilitating trade or promoting activity and that
this level should be offered only for a short period
of time and thus is an excess and can be expected
to move. For example, when a new, higher price
produces a substantially lower level of activity, it
signals to the producer that, for the moment, a
lower price (or a corrective marketing strategy
such as advertising) is needed if sales of the
product or service are to pick up.

Similarly, if the producer, for whatever reason,
lowers the price beyond the point where he can
make an equitable profit, he will soon shut off the
availability of the product at the unreasonably low
price and will charge more.

*Time*

Time, the market component few participants
rely on when making trading decisions, allows us
to measure the degree of change between need
and price in the marketplace. It is a known

constant, a measurement which participants inadvertently use when determining value through transactional data. Time impacts trade by regulating the duration during which buying (consuming) and selling (producing) can take place.

Because competition to buy low and sell high is present, the market, in facilitating trade, uses price to promote opportunity and uses time to regulate how long that opportunity will last. The market insures that when price promotes opportunity to the point of reaching an excess, that price is held in check. The market continually uses time to regulate itself throughout its structure.

Examples of how time regulates price activity can be seen in the previous illustrations showing how price promotes activity. In the post-holiday sale, while the department store management was willing to sell at prices half of those charged prior to the holidays, management was not willing to offer this "below value" opportunity for long, but only until the current inventory was sold. Had the store extended the opportunity to purchase merchandise into what is considered the regular shopping season, the lower post-holiday sale prices would soon be considered the new value area. This is something no retailer would want to see. Retail stores and other producers/sellers use the lower excess price to promote activity only so long as it fulfills the purpose behind the excess price. Interestingly, the sharper the price reduction — or the farther the offered price is below value — the shorter the time period the opportunity will be available.

Likewise, the example of the resort hotel illustrates that time regulates activity. Higher prices promoted activity among producers, thereby attracting new hotels. The high prices charged first by the lone hotel and then by the new hotel market entrants were in hindsight an excess which persisted only until the demand for hotel space was met and exceeded. This activity (rising land values and hotel construction) continued until it went too high (hotels saturated the demand) and activity at the high prices was shut off. Thus, while the hotel near the resort park could temporarily charge prices considered above value, the market's excess promoted this opportunity to others, so that the hotel was not able to sustain the high prices and low vacancy status for long. Thus, through a long timeframe, time regulates the high price activity and controls it.

**Conclusion:** The components which combine to create a marketplace interact in the following way. Participants, each with his own timeframe for operating, and each affected by market-imposed forcing points, either enter or do not enter the market at the most recent price. This collective activity controls and regulates itself through its allocation of price — higher prices advertise for sellers, while lower prices advertise for buyers — and time. Thus it yields types of natural organization which, in producing excesses to test market acceptance, produce balance and provide information.

The obvious conclusion is a major breakthrough for anyone who understands the market's inherent and observable logic. The conclusion that the market acts logically flies in the face of the conventional wisdom which says that price is the only mechanism that the market uses to balance or ration supply and demand. (Introductory economic theory asserts this, econometric models are built assuming it, and many investors and traders have experienced setbacks believing it.) When participants focus on price and price alone, they simply cannot obtain an understanding of the underlying strength or weakness of the market, the market's condition. Thus, an analysis of a price versus price is inherently narrowly focused and, taken out of context, is oftentimes virtually meaningless. Yet it is this assumption — measuring a price against another price — upon which moving average, relative strength, stochastic and other technically based indicators are modeled.

# Chapter 4

# Principles of Auctions

AUCTION: A sale by increase of bids. A public sale in which property or items of merchandise are sold to the highest bidder.

DUTCH AUCTION: An auction in which the auctioneer opens with a high price and lowers it until a buyer is found.

From the days of early Rome, when soldiers divided the spoils of war by holding auctions on the battlefield, the auction process has been the most effective means of determining the fair value of property. The reason, in a word, is competition — a multitude of buyers competing with one another, bidding up the price of the item being auctioned until price moves high enough that only one buyer is left.

Auctions are used extensively in everyday competitive market situations. Consider the overbooked flight, which forces airlines in the U.S. to compensate "bumped" passengers with a free flight. To determine who gets bumped, airline officials hold an auction at the terminal gate, offering free tickets as an inducement to passengers who will willingly give up their seat to take a later flight. Those passengers with important appointments to keep are constrained by their timeframe and are unwilling to be compensated for missing their flight with a free ticket. But passengers who have a longer timeframe from which to operate (i.e., no pressing appointments) have the luxury of feeling comfortable waiting for another flight and can be compensated for doing so.

The type of auction process known as open outcry has come to symbolize capitalistic free markets at their purest and most competitive. The open outcry which occurs on the floor of a financial exchange is a subset of the universe of competitive auctions. Therefore, an examination of the process behind an ordinary competitive auction reveals insights and a background helpful for understanding the internal workings of the financial markets.

## All markets are auction markets and are of two types.

*PASSIVE AUCTIONS:* In a passive auction, participants select from a range of prices that are already determined.

*ACTIVE AUCTIONS:* In an active auction, participants develop the range of prices themselves (as a part of the auction process).

Examples of passive auction markets can be found in the unorganized markets in which we participate as everyday consumers. In a department store or grocery store, for example, the consumer is offered a wide selection of prices (usually varying with quality) to choose from. Watches at the department store may be offered over a sizeable price range. In the grocery store, even such staples as beef may vary in price dramatically. This type of auction gives the consumer an opportunity to select, from a range of predetermined prices, the price at which he wants to do business.

In active auctions, on the other hand, the

consumer plays an active role in determining
what price will be attached to a particular item. At
a traditional auction the auctioneer acts as agent
for the seller of the property. Potential buyers bid
on the property, raising their bids as the process
proceeds, until all but one bidder remains willing
to bid. He "wins" and the property is his.

Another type of active auction is termed a
"dutch auction." In this process sellers offer their
(similar) property at successively lower prices
until a potential buyer accepts one of the offers.

Aside from auctions of art, collectibles and so
forth, many transactions regularly occur using
active auctions for price discovery. An example
which illustrates the types of auctions with which
we are all familiar is the housing market. When a
prospective buyer begins his search for a house,
he inquires as to the price range that houses in his
chosen area have actually been selling (trading)
for. This helps him to establish what is value for
that area. A passive auction takes place as the
potential buyer selects from the many houses for
sale on the market. Subsequently, in the
negotiations which will determine the final sale
price of the house, the buyer will keep raising his
bid incrementally (traditional active auction), as
the seller lowers his offer incrementally (dutch
active auction).

It is significant to note that in an active one-
directional auction, the auction begins with an
obvious imbalance signifying unfairness to one
side of the consumer-producer equation: many
ready buyers at the opening bid, and only one
ready seller. As the auction proceeds, prices move
directionally until the vast imbalance begins to
subside, as fewer and fewer are willing to bid. (See
illustration, next page.) Finally, as the market
moves from imbalance and unfair prices toward

balance and a fair price, there is but one lone
buyer bidding on the lone object being auctioned.
A fair price has been discovered, according to the
willingness of the participants present at the
auction to respond or not respond based on the
price movement.

### Financial Markets Are Auctions

This chapter has examined traditional auctions
because the auction process which occurs daily
on the floors of the financial exchanges operates
in essentially the same manner. In keeping with a
financial market's sole purpose — facilitating
trade — the market employs both traditional (low
to high) and dutch active auction processes, in a
combination referred to as "dual auction process."
That is, in a stock, futures or options market, the
purpose of price is to neutralize any imbalance
between buyer and seller. When an imbalance of
more buyers than sellers occurs, price moves up
to advertise for sellers. If price moves up to a high
enough level that an imbalance of more sellers
than buyers is discovered, price moves back down
to find buyers. Important to note is that the higher
price moves up to encourage sellers to enter the
market, the fewer buyers are encouraged from
participating. So, in order to fulfill its purpose, the
market will move back down to involve as many
participants as possible.

The action of trade moving back and forth
between high and low prices is referred to as
**rotation**. Price rotates, auctions up and auctions
down, advertising for sellers and buyers to fulfill
the market's purpose of facilitating trade, at the
same time discovering the market's collective view
of current fair price.

As the market's natural behavior unfolds,
another very important function occurs. This
process of the market rotating back and forth

from high prices to low and back again to high, etc., often produces what we term excess prices. In other words, markets tend to overcompensate for an apparent imbalance. This propensity for price to go too far too fast often creates temporary benchmarks, references that price went too far up in rallying, creating a significant imbalance caused by increased selling. Thus, the excess provides participants with information which indicates that the market has gone high enough to go too high, and that the high is an excess.

However, the market does not always produce these benchmarks or reference points for all to see. When changes in price occur that are so small and subtle that a gross imbalance is not created and activity is not shut off violently, there is no overcompensation or excess in the marketplace. In this condition the market may trend or show slow and consistent directional continuation. Thus, when the market is facilitating trade, it is either going to be overcompensating for imbalance and hence displaying excess or else operating with slight, subtle imbalance which produces no excess, indicating the possibility of steady directional movement.

**Conclusion:** Auction markets are all around us. They are understandable and behave in a logical manner. Financial markets, a subset of active auction markets, demonstrate the same logical and understandable operational behavior. Whether it is an art auction at Christie's or an IBM out-of-the-money call option, both consumer (buyer) and producer (seller) are interested in either buying or selling the maximum amount at an advantageous price. Because of the endless quest to facilitate trade on the part of all participants, the price continually tests for market acceptance as determined through an imbalance of buyers to seller, probing higher and then lower prices, again and again. In order to discover balance, the market needs to go too high and too low to find an area that is fair for both parties over a period of time. This rotating activity produces overcompensations which in retrospect become considered either fair or unfair prices: fair if the level of overcompensation results in a price level that is accepted over time, unfair if the level of overcompensation attracts competition and thus does not trade over time. These excesses on both sides give the market its natural organization and provide information to participants. Thus, in the market's natural order, it produces a top extreme, a bottom extreme, and a fair area. All three provide empirical benchmarks to market participants.

# Chapter 5

# Observations Defined and Characterized: Market Background and Definitions

The market's production of two extremes bounding an accepted price area occurs routinely. Its presence or absence allows the participant to see the financial market's expanded role, that of an information generator. The market consistently promulgates its current definition of value — the fact of like transactions occurring, over time, in an area of similar prices. This information allows all participants to recognize disparities in the price-value relationship.

This chapter will tie together many of the points made in the previous chapters regarding how markets operate and what information is generated. The following observations form the methodological basis for understanding current market conditions.

**Observation #1: Market participants gain confidence as time passes.**

On a given day, a financial market's volatility varies depending on the length of time the market has been trading. Soon after the opening, the concerns and needs of the dominant participants

are brought into focus. The market opens at what
the dominant participants consider a fair price
based on their interpretation of up-to-the-
moment news events, government reports, or
other information outside the market relating to
current conditions, real or rumored, and how they
may affect value.

From here the price discovery process starts.
The (often news-related) concerns and (hedge or
speculative positioning-related) needs of the
participants dominant on the opening are
neutralized as they transact. Those who wish to
buy and sell do so, and the market finds balance
in a price area which is fair for all currently active
participants. Since the market has only just
opened, short timeframe participants do not have
a high level of confidence in the condition of the
market. New participants can at any time enter
the market either as net buyers, net sellers or a
mixture of both. If either net buying or net selling
does enter, the market's fragile balance will be
upset and a new price level will be found. The
speed and volatility with which this new price area
is tested depend on the magnitude of participation
by the new entrants. If small net buying comes in,
the market will rally somewhat; if large orders to
buy "at the market" come in, the rally will be more
pronounced.

The new entrants whose buy and sell orders
were not present on the opening tend to enter the
market shortly after the opening. The more
anxious the participants, the earlier they tend to
act. By the end of the first hour, the market should
have attracted a large percentage of the
participants' orders.

After the first hour's trade, the market's initial
balance has been set and the market-makers
have more confidence than just after the opening.

They have seen the orders of both buyers and sellers come in and get served, moving price usually both up and down. They take note of the high prices where major selling was attracted and the low prices where major buying came in. The market-makers now have reference points for the prices at which they can expect selling and buying. They know the extent of range containment for the present, have some reference as to the degree of balance or imbalance in the market, and can identify the range of prevailing market prices over the first hour of trade.

Once the initial balance has been set, the market can be said to be in balance over the short term, but not necessarily over the longer term. Price remains temporarily within the initial range until the market's balance is upset by an influx of either new net buyers or net sellers. This new imbalance changes the market's condition, and price will then normally move directionally to neutralize the developing imbalance.

**Observation #2: Observing clusters of transactions recurring at similar price levels over time leads one to a general understanding of value.**

Given the observations made in the previous chapters, we can identify a significant market behavior as it is occurring: that certain clusters of transactions tend to congregate around near-equal prices. Because we are aware of the inherent self-interest which motivates collective market activity, we know that if transactions at a given price level recur over time, that price is being accepted as fair for both buyer and seller.

All markets, regardless of the timeframe over which they are organized, regularly display a readable preference for a certain contiguous range of prices while rejecting price levels above and below this fair area. We refer to that price or the cluster of near equal prices as **value** — the market's collective expression of currently fair prices — while associating transactional prices that do not recur, and therefore are not reinforced by time, as unfair prices, or prices away from value. Most informed participants either consciously or unconsciously associate this price range — the area where prices recur over time — with value.

This is a major "edge" the floor market participant has over the random walk community: he understands that

**prices recurring over time yield value
(Price + Time = Value).**

Understanding the existence of the market's daily self-described value is a major step toward appreciating the market's informational role, introduced in the last chapter.

As mentioned earlier, the most significant condition of a market revolves around the extent to which it facilitates trade, which is defined by transactional volume measured over equal time increments. The vast majority of volume will lie with those prices seen with time. Thus, volume will almost invariably be concentrated in the value area, while the price areas above and below value which were rejected as unfair will display a comparatively smaller amount of transactional volume.

Significantly, monitoring the value area can aid in determining the direction and strength of a trend — the ever-important signal as to whether the market is accepting higher or lower prices over time versus not being receptive to price change. The general direction of value areas of similar width is more important to note than simple price fluctuations. An emerging trend can often be discerned much more quickly by observing directional changes in value than through traditional technical tools.

**Observation #3: To understand the condition of a market at any given time, it is important to categorize the market's participants by their timeframe and to monitor their behavior.**

A market will exhibit current conditions. For example, the market can trend, or it can meander in a directionless sideways movement. When markets trend, the trend can be very strong and directional; or it can be moderately strong, indicating a zigzag or ebb-and-flow type of pattern where higher highs and higher lows are achieved over time; or the trend can be stalling, with the market about to move violently in the opposite direction to the recent trend. Importantly, there are discernible underlying behavioral patterns which will indicate whether the market can expect to change from its current condition.

Market behavior is nothing more than human behavior responding or not responding to current price. Thus, to understand the market's current condition, and to be able to reasonably determine whether current conditions will continue and for how long, we must study the people who participate in the financial markets.

Participants can be grouped into those with shorter timeframes and those with longer timeframes. It is the entry of the longer timeframe participants that upsets a market's balance, causing a rise in price over the short term. Their continued net entry — that is, more net buying than selling, or more net selling without buying to balance it — over a period of time will cause a market to trend directionally. The challenge of the market participant seeking to determine the direction of the trend is to monitor the presence and level of anxiety of long timeframe participants either as net buyers or net sellers.

The percentage mix of short timeframe to long timeframe participants in a market affects the degree of volatility the market experiences, while also providing structure to the market. Active long timeframe buyers will buffer the market at prices low enough to be attractive for them while the presence of active long timeframe sellers will prevent the market from going straight up, as higher prices will attract them to sell. This type of condition — a market where both long timeframe buyers and long timeframe sellers are active — would behave differently from a market where one group predominates. We term such a market a **two timeframe market**, since both long timeframe buying and selling groups are present and active.

In a two timeframe market, price, rotating up and down, shuts off the currently dominant activity, and at the same time advertises for opposite activity. In other words, as the dominant buying activity enters the market, price moves up to shut off the buying and attract selling, which, if sucessful, will make the market move off its highs. Because the long timeframe seller sells at sufficiently high prices while the long timeframe buyer buys at sufficiently low prices, the day's high-low range can be expected to remain contained.

Compare this to a situation where only one group, either long timeframe buyers or sellers, enters the market without the other group. This condition, which we describe as a **one timeframe market**, can be expected to move directionally rather than to be contained. Despite occasional

"One Timeframe Market"

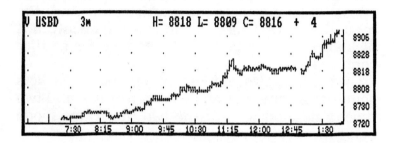

"Two Timeframe Market"

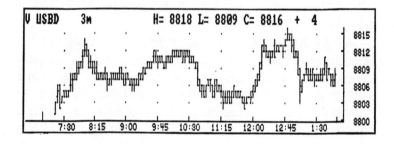

pauses, the market usually continues directionally in this mode in the absence of the opposite long timeframe participant. And the more the market moves, the more momentum it picks up and the greater the chance for further continuation.

Over the course of any week most markets comprise a combination of one timeframe and two timeframe modes, with the two timeframe mode being most common.

**Observation #4: Balance is the essence of the market. The degree to which a market is imbalanced will determine its ability to sustain a trend.**

We are familiar with balance and imbalance as seen in everyday markets. We know how to adjust to each and we also understand the inherent ability of markets to self-correct when not in balance. For instance, the restaurant which continually has long lines of patrons waiting for a table informs us that a meal there probably equals price below value. The restaurant could either expand capacity or raise prices to adjust to current imbalanced conditions.

All markets are balancing mechanisms, with price being the variable that reacts to an imbalance among buyers and sellers by moving directionally to neutralize what was an unfair situation at that time. Thus, price changes occur for a logical reason, fulfill a purpose, and reflect the condition of the market. It is important to observe and understand the collective activity of long and short timeframe buyers and sellers around a given price. We are particularly interested in the behavior of the long timeframe buyers and sellers, because their degree of participation reveals the extent to which a market is out of balance (trending). Significantly, this condition of imbalance — trend — does not subside immediately.

The group of participants who don't have to transact but choose to — the long timeframe participants — have the power to cause the market to trend, the result of imbalance. The entry of these participants to the market, as we shall see later in the book, is an observable phenomenon. And it is important to witness the degree of imbalance they create if we are to know whether the market is poised to trend.

An important concept to keep in mind is that any response or change produces new surrounding circumstances, or trade-offs. It is therefore critical to monitor the market as changes in price occur or as the day, the week, and the month unfold. An information flow comes from seeing how both long timeframe buyer and seller accept changes in both price and time.

A market can either be in balance, or out of balance. An out of balance market usually continues to be out of balance until either sufficient directional price changes occur or sufficient time passes. Either or both will diffuse imbalance. Increasingly higher price within a balanced market condition is not an attractive situation for one who expects trend continuation. In contrast, increasingly higher price with substantial imbalance is a condition which would tend to indicate continuation. The same is of course true for decreasing price with balance versus decreasing price with substantial imbalance.

Concentrating on the degree of balance or imbalance currently exhibited by a market leads one to recognize behavior patterns as they relate to value. While to the unobservant outsider the reoccurrence of manias and panics adds to the mystery associated with markets, they are in fact merely a reflection of everyday human emotionalism which causes the imbalanced condition which always precedes these headline-grabbing events. The high degree of imbalance is regularly repeated and can be detected as it slowly develops, ahead of the headlines. As a market condition, it can be readily understood.

# SECTION TWO:

# Organizing Markets to Read Market-Generated Information

This section will present two methods of organization which will more fully display the non-chaotic order with which the markets have functioned for centuries. These formats will allow the market to be observed in a logical framework. When used confidently, they should enhance the trader's ability to de-emphasize the emotional decision-making that markets are famous for fomenting. This should help him to dispassionately gauge the market's current conditions: the extent of trade facilitation and the degree of balance or imbalance present. Finally, use of these formats will enable the trader to gauge a very important market factor, namely, the level of activity of the dominant longer timeframe outside participants at various price levels.

# Chapter 6

# The Importance of Assessing Value

Consider the type of market-generated information most people deem important. When asked, most bystanders would respond that the most recent price is what they use as their yardstick when evaluating the worth of their goods. Yet, as those close to the market know, the price of the most recent transaction in and of itself is of little use in formulating an informed buy-sell decision. It is the relationship of price to value — the development of price over time — that provides the greatest and most important information, defining the type of opportunity one is facing.

The bible of the financial world, *Securities Analysis*, by Graham and Dodd, stresses that understanding and assessing current market price as it relates to current market value should be the ultimate goal of the portfolio manager. Their seminal work advocates analyzing the company's fundamentals (balance sheets, income statements, assets, etc.), information that is generated at least quarterly and often monthly. This regular flow of information — outside the marketplace — should be analyzed and combined with knowledge of the current risk-free rate of return, allowing the investor/analyst to ascertain a company's value. (It is important to remember

43

that value is never a specific price, but always a range of prices.)

The idea is that the stock's price could either be trading below, within or above current value at any one point in time. It is knowledge of where the stock's current price is relative to current value which defines the opportunity. Thus, the so-called corporate raider who does his homework well, remains patient and only enters when he is buying price substantially below value usually wins, buying stocks that appreciate, allowing him either to sell them at higher prices or take over the company. The success of the Icahn, Pickens, Jacobs, Steinberg mode of investment is a testament to the analytical validity of Graham and Dodd, and obviously is yet another annoyance to the efficient market theorists who posit that price equals value once a stock, future or option is traded on an exchange floor.

As mentioned before, successful floor traders, participants with shorter time horizons, use a decision-making process virtually identical to the Graham and Dodd approach, yet based on a different information flow. Rather than using information outside the marketplace, the savvy trader, either consciously or unconsciously, relies on market-generated information to ascertain the stock or financial instrument's current value. He then looks to take advantage of price when it deviates from current value, just as do Warren Buffett and the successful investors mentioned above. The successful floor trader, whether specialist, options market-maker or futures pit local, consciously or unconsciously applies this knowledge and experience to his decision-making process. The floor trader's awareness of a strong price/time relationship representing value is knowledge that differentiates him from the vast

majority of financial market participants away
from the floor.

### The Market's Self-Defined Value

An understanding of how the market currently
defines value can augment the decision-making
process, whether the decision-maker is a portfolio
manager, institutional trader, or anyone else
actively involved in financial markets. Any
portfolio manager schooled in market logic applies
this tool every time he or she wishes to buy or sell
a particular instrument on either fundamental,
technical or asset allocation grounds. Again, we
are simply following the recommendations of
Graham and Dodd: conduct analysis which
defines value. The market in individual equities
offers the flow of information (balance sheets,
income statements, etc.) that Graham and Dodd
require, but fixed income, currency and physical
futures markets do not. Of course, it could be
argued that government status reports such as
money supply, balance of trade payments,
producer price index, unemployment, etc., are
balance sheets for these markets, but avowed
Graham and Doddists would find it difficult to
ascertain value from them. Nevertheless, the fact
that the market defines value by the collective
transactional expression of all currently involved
participants allows the participant to seek to
exploit opportunities when price is away from
value.

Significantly, changes in price occur quickly,
and can be relatively dramatic, whereas changes
in value, particularly when viewed over the longer
term, tend to occur in a much more deliberate,
steady and orderly fashion. Price has a very
straightforward relationship to value. Price can be
above value, within value (i.e., unchanged value)
or below value. A range of prices can be composed

of a mixture of those above, within and below
value.

After ascertaining the proximity of the most
recent price to value, the informed participant
looks at the type of response present. For
example, if the most recent transactions produced
prices above value, no activity could occur, selling
activity could occur, or buying activity could
occur. In other words, the market's collective
response to a price above value can be absent,
thereby displaying a lack of facilitation at that
time, or it could be the expected response, a
selling response, or it could be opposite of what
would be expected, showing anxious buyers as a
group were initiating transactions above value.

# Chapter 7

# Grouping Participants According to Timeframe

To measure the degree of balance in the market, we re-examine the issue of the participants who act in the market.

It was previously noted that in an everyday market situation participants could theoretically be categorized along a spectrum according to their timeframe. The most impatient to buy would be the shortest timeframe buyers. Next to them would come those who needed to buy very shortly, perhaps in the next day or so. Next to them would be those who expected to make purchases during the upcoming week, and so on. The further out the buyers are on this timeframe spectrum, the longer the timeframe and the more significant their activity to directional price movement, because although they do not have a pressing need to transact, the fact that long timeframers are doing so spells imbalance. In other words, Adam Smith's "Invisible Hand," to which he (Smith, Kondratieff and others) attributes any and every market's self-correcting mechanism, is nothing more than the net group of longer timeframe participants pursuing their self-interest.

In order to deduce, isolate and identify the presence of the invisible hand (the longer timeframe activity) we must be able to economically organize or further categorize

participants according to their timeframe. We do
so by essentially creating a model which organizes
market participants into two groups:

    1. Individuals who intend to trade today,
    whom we will call "day timeframe."

    2. Individuals who intend to trade at
    some point, not necessarily today. The
    latter group has a timeframe beyond and
    other than the day. We will call them
    "other" timeframe.

It must be remembered that participant
timeframes are not static. Individuals voluntarily
change their timeframe, and price movement
combined with changes in participant
circumstances can force a change in timeframe.
Using the above definitions, our ability to discern
current conditions will not be unduly hindered by
this.

We have now two clearly defined categories
(buyers versus sellers, and day timeframe versus
other timeframe) which we can use to organize
market participants. When we can group market
participants by these categories, and understand
the implications of our findings, we become much
more informed participants. We know that the
probable behavior of a buyer differs from that of a
seller, and to the extent that we know the
conditions of the market are such that at
currently low prices unrequited buyers
outnumber the few sellers, the obvious imbalance
will mean prices will not fall and have a good
chance of rising.

The next point to be made regarding participant
characteristics centers around how certain
knowledge of current conditions can allow one to
have what might be termed "reasonable
expectations." The goal of attaining reasonable
expectations comes into play in any logical model

where the future is uncertain. For instance, when playing blackjack with a single deck, the adept card counter may have a reasonable expectation of being dealt a 10 or royalty if a certain number of hands have been played without these cards coming up. The more hands dealt without these cards coming up, the greater his confidence in his expectation. Note that he does not predict the future, but makes decisions based on probable outcomes, reasonable expectations given knowledge of current conditions.

When analyzing current conditions, it is key to understand the extent to which a market is out of balance. This is because a trend is caused by one of these two groups continuing to enter the market, creating an imbalanced situation that price neutralizes through directional movement. The prime focus of one who seeks reasonable expectations, then, involves whether either the other timeframe buyer or the other timeframe seller can be expected to enter at a given price.

Consider the following:

**Other timeframe traders** transact with day timeframe traders.

**Day timeframe traders** transact with other day timeframe traders.

**Other timeframe buyers** do not transact at the same price at the same time with other timeframe sellers.

To the extent that current imbalance can be attributed to significant activity on the part of one other timeframe group, we can expect that the market will not move sharply in the opposite direction any time within the next half hour time period and usually longer. This is because such price movement could only be caused by the entry of the opposite other timeframe group. In other words, a strong new high made after the initial range is the result of imbalance caused by the other timeframe buyer. When the new high occurs, one can reasonably expect that the market will either remain in the area defined by the current high-low range, or else it will continue to move up, as the condition of the market — buying imbalance — either subsides or continues. The odds are not in favor of the market breaking sharply within the next half hour or so after the market makes a new high, since the other timeframe buyer and the other timeframe seller do not transact with each other at the same price at the same time.

Another point to be made is that the day timeframe participant and the other timeframe participant differ in their reasons for participating. The day timeframe participant looks only for a "fair" price, a price where volume has been transacted, due to his need to trade on the day. He generally uses close benchmarks of market-generated information such as an imbalance of buyers and sellers, and often reacts (and overreacts) to a news event or the release of fundamental data. Day timeframe participants are most active and produce most of the volume. Thus when reacting to a news event or a report they often can produce a tremendous amount of volatility and major directional price movements. These report reactions often move quickly only to spring back during that day, often shortly after the report.

In contrast, the other timeframe participant is not looking for a fair price as much as he seeks a price away from value or an advantageous opportunity in value. The other timeframe participant is usually not a significant portion of the average day's volume. When this group is dominant, the day no longer remains average, since the resulting imbalance must be neutralized by directional price movement. Responding to price movements that offer price away from value opportunities, the other timeframe trader is often a buffering factor in the market when a news event causes the day timeframe trader to overreact and move price too far. This is why sharp directional price changes often can change the condition of the market to a regrouping or test phase, while small, incremental changes usually can continue directionally.

Any imbalance — caused by the long or short timeframe trader — has the possibility of causing directional price change. Such a price move, if sustained, creates the new fair range of prices, a new area of balance. In other words, when the other timeframe trader does not buffer the market, which causes price to spring back to value, the new area is accepted as fair value.

Obviously, the group of those who participate in a market will be composed of a mix of the two timeframe groups. And it is the interplay between these two groups which creates the ebb and flow of the market.

# Chapter 8

# The Bell Curve: Giving Structure and Meaning to the Market

The structure that allows the participant to extract the most meaning from a market's price fluctuation is normal distribution, the bell curve. With the bell curve, seemingly "chaotic" activity is placed in an understandable format which defines current value. The bell curve organizes price on a vertical axis and time on the horizontal axis. Price therefore becomes a variable measured by time, a constant.

For every exchange-traded financial instrument thus far studied — stocks, options, financial and commodity futures markets — the phenomenon of a bell curve regularly results on the vast majority of days. The bell curve, an organizing tool that is used extensively outside the financial markets to provide statistically significant visual representations of reality, displays an area of collective acceptance, usually bounded by an extreme on each side. Applied to a financial market, the area of price recurring over time (the first standard deviation; 70% of the total volume on the day) defines market acceptance or value to floor traders and others looking to garner market-generated information. Those prices above and below this value area that are rejected by the

## THE BELL CURVE

| P | 89.05 | A |
|---|-------|---|
| R | 89.04 | A |
| I | 89.03 | A |
| C | 89.02 | AK |
| E | 89.01 | AD |
|   | 89.00 | BDGKL |
|   | 88.31 | BDFGJKL |
|   | 88.30 | BCDFGJKL |
|   | 88.29 | BCDEFGJL |
|   | 88.28 | BCDEFGJL |
|   | 88.27 | BCDEFGHJ |
|   | 88.26 | BCDEFGHJ |
|   | 88.25 | BCDEFGHIJ |
|   | 88.24 | BCDEHIJ |
|   | 88.23 | BDEHI |
|   | 88.22 | DEHI |
|   | 88.21 | DEH |
|   | 88.20 | E |
|   | 88.19 | E |

© 1984 CECT

## TIME PERIODS:

"A" = 08:00 TO 08:30
"B" = 08:30 TO 09:00
"C" = 09:00 TO 09:30
"D" = 09:30 TO 10:00
"E" = 10:00 TO 10:30
"F" = 10:30 TO 11:00
"G" = 11:00 TO 11:30
"H" = 11:30 TO 12:00
"I" = 12:00 TO 12:30
"J" = 12:30 TO 13:00
"K" = 13:00 TO 13:30
"L" = 13:30 TO 14:00

market are seen as unfair prices, prices away from value. The insight that stems from this realization is that the market, organized over whatever time increments, regularly displays a readable collective preference of prices.

On any given day, the low extreme (price below value and without time) is caused because lower prices have attracted increased competition among buyers, while the high extreme (price above value and without time) indicates that higher prices have attracted competition among sellers. Thus, to the extent that the market continues to return over time to, for instance, the low prices of the day, the market would not have a buying extreme; this would

indicate imbalance to the sell side due to lack of competition among buyers. If in this situation the market at the same time displays a well-defined extreme at the higher range of prices that day, a trader in tune with the market might remark, "This market is weak." Assuming the overall trend in value is down, he would be opting more for being short or neutral the market, rather than long. The point is that the bell curve not only displays the degree of trade facilitation but also visually portrays imbalance. In this example it would display an imbalance caused by an oversupply of ready sellers relative to those willing to buy at current levels.

### The Invisible Hand Creates Imbalance

If the market is a balancing mechanism, all significant price movement must occur in reaction to an imbalance of net buying or selling. Thus, organizing the market via a bell curve illustrates imbalance, to the extent that changes in value occur more slowly than the volatile changes in price. Analyzing a series of profiles of a particular market augments longer term decision-making in

assessing the direction and strength of a longer
term trend, the probable directional movement of
a stock reacting to an upcoming news
announcement, etc. In other words, the other
timeframe group, the so-called invisible hand,
creates imbalance, and continued imbalance
creates a trend. To focus on the dominant other
timeframe group is our goal.

Before doing this, however, we should consider
the nature of how the market organizes itself on a
daily basis, a topic developed in Observation #1 in
Chapter 5. As we said, the market opens and early
on seeks to find an initial balance, a range of
prices where fairness can be established, given
the current flow of orders created by the mix of
day and other timeframe traders. In order to do
this the market probes high and low, hopefully too
high and too low, thereby setting references with
these excesses. As the day unfolds, the conditions
of the market stay the same or change, and price
may extend in either direction (or, very rarely, in
both directions). If extension occurs, the
benchmarks may be removed as the day's price
range unfolds and is established.

When examined both from a shorter-term
perspective and over a large sample size, three
areas on the bell curve define the degree of
imbalance caused by the other timeframe
participants or, when they are not active, the fact
of relative balance. The three indicators, which
may or may not be present on a given profile, are:

**Buying and/or selling extremes**
**Buying and/or selling range extensions**
**A visually skewed distribution, indicated by
time price opportunity (or "TPO") imbalance**

The presence of buying and/or selling extremes,
range extensions, and visual imbalance along

**Illustrated Other Timeframe Market Activity:**
**Extremes and Range Extensions**

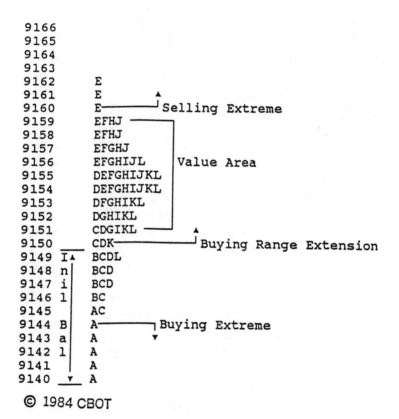

```
9166
9165
9164
9163
9162        E
9161        E              ▲
9160        E──────────────┘ Selling Extreme
9159        EFHJ ──┐
9158        EFHJ   │
9157        EFGHJ  │
9156        EFGHIJL    │ Value Area
9155        DEFGHIJKL  │
9154        DEFGHIJKL  │
9153        DFGHIKL    │
9152        DGHIKL     │
9151        CDGIKL ──┘        ▲
9150  ___   CDK──────────────┘ Buying Range Extension
9149 I▲     BCDL
9148 n│     BCD
9147 i│     BCD
9146 l│     BC
9145  │     AC
9144 B│     A──────────┐ Buying Extreme
9143 a│     A          ▼
9142 l│     A
9141  │     A
9140  ▼ ___ A
```

© 1984 CBOT

with an assessment of the degree of trade facilitation defines the current condition of the market. These tools do nothing more than measure imbalance, which is the goal of any market participant in any market, organized or unorganized. Each indicates that imbalance — increased competition caused by the other timeframe net group — is present. The more pronounced a buying and/or selling extreme, range extension and/or a visually imbalanced profile, the greater the degree of imbalance present.

Several assumptions are made in coming to the conclusion that the trend can be deduced from these three indicators.

1) Over the short term, competition of either net buying and net selling creates an imbalance, which is then neutralized by price moving directionally, thereby creating a fair and more balanced situation.

2) Day timeframe participants are always present in a viable market, but it is the entry of other timeframe participants competing to either buy or sell which creates the additional pressure, the net imbalance.

3) The day timeframe participants as a group are extremely quick to react to a net imbalance. They react by adjusting the price at which they will trade, simply because it is in their own best interest to do so.

In a future chapter, we will study an interpretation of the bell curve based on, among other things, the presence of buying and/or selling extremes and range extensions. These indicators can forewarn against one of the greatest frustrations the trader faces: an unpredictable news event which dramatically alters price.

It is impossible to know all news events that will affect any given market, but the bell curve (analyzed from the standpoint of the degree of trade facilitation, buying and selling extremes, range extensions, and TPO imbalance) is a tool which provides insight into the possible nature of an upcoming event.

Consider the following example of how a series of profiles of Union Carbide stock measured the degree of imbalance which existed directly prior to the what was to the interested stockholder well-publicized board meeting in May, 1988. (See illustration.)

Following the October crash, Union Carbide (UK hereafter) traded in the mid-$20's, and in the final two weeks of March through the week of May 6th, UK traded quietly in a narrow range of $22 1/2 to $24. Note the market action of the 16th, when UK posted its lowest trade volume in recent months. Note that on this day price moved lower over time and was accepted. On the 17th, UK spent most of the day building value in the 23 1/8 to 3/8 area, but experienced a late break which extended price south in M and N periods. Clearly, one could conclude that price was moving lower over time on this day, and that this market did not portray a balanced (normal bell curve) market situation, but rather one that was dominated by net selling.

The markets are a subset of the physical universe and as such are regulated by the laws of physics; just as any object in motion continues in motion while an object in rest tends to stay in rest, so too with markets. When a market is out of balance (net selling outweighed by buying or vice versa) price must move directionally far enough to

UNION CARBIDE PRICE DISTRIBUTION     **KNIGHT-RIDDER TRADECENTER**
MAY 16 - 19, 1988

| PRICE | TIME BRACKET | | | |
|---|---|---|---|---|
| | May 16 | May 17 | May 18 | May 19 |
| 23.7 | | | | |
| 23.6 | | | | |
| 23.5 | | B | | |
| 23.4 | | BC | | |
| 23.3 | BCDEFKLMN | CDEF | | |
| 23.2 | BCDEFGHIJKLMNP | CDEFGHIJKL | | |
| 23.1 | GHIJ | FGHIJKLM | | |
| 23.0 | | KM | | |
| 22.7 | | MN | | |
| 22.6 | | MN | B | |
| 22.5 | | NP | BCDEF | |
| 22.4 | | NP | BCDEF | |
| 22.3 | | | F | |
| 22.2 | | | F | |
| 22.1 | | | FGI | |
| 22.0 | | | GHI | |
| 21.7 | | | GHIK | |
| 21.6 | | | KLMN | |
| 21.5 | | | IJKLMN | |
| 21.4 | | | JN | |
| 21.3 | | | N | |
| 21.2 | | | N | |
| 21.1 | | | N | |
| 21.0 | | | N | |
| 20.7 | | | NP | |
| 20.6 | | | NP | |
| 20.5 | | | | |
| 20.4 | | | | |
| 20.3 | | | | |
| 20.2 | | | | |
| 20.1 | | | | |
| 20.0 | | | | |
| 19.7 | | | | |
| 19.6 | | | | |
| 19.5 | | | | |
| 19.4 | | | | |
| 19.3 | | | | |
| 19.2 | | | | |
| 19.1 | | | | |
| 19.0 | | | | |
| 18.7 | | | | |
| 18.6 | | | | |
| 18.5 | | | | |
| 18.4 | | | | |
| 18.3 | | | | M |
| 18.2 | | | | KLMNP |
| 18.1 | | | | GJKLMNP |
| 18.0 | | | | DFGHIJKL |
| 17.7 | | | | DEFGHIJ |
| 17.6 | | | © 1984 CBOT | DEF |

remove that imbalance. Remember, market imbalance is indicative of unfairness. In other words, market imbalances do not self-correct without either a slow subsiding of the imbalance or a directional price movement.

It was the move initiated on the 18th that brought concern to many analysts and portfolio managers. Between 11:30 and 12:00 Eastern standard time, prices began plummeting, obviously due to a wave of sell orders. This imbalanced condition did not subside but dominated the session, as subsequent half hours scored lower lows and lower highs. We label this pattern a **trend day.** A pattern familiar to all active traders, it illustrates a directional move caused by the highest degree of imbalance possible in a market. It is interesting to point out that even for the analyst following this stock, the move came apparently without a news announcement as provocation.

Late in the afternoon of the 18th, the veil was lifted: Union Carbide announced a dividend cut of some 43%. The following morning, the stock opened late some $3 lower, representing a devaluation of a major Fortune 500 company of 23% over only 36 hours.

A more in-depth analysis of the stock movement prior to the break would explain more clearly why such a downward movement would not be a surprise for someone who was "reading the tape," organizing the market via the bell curve. This example was introduced at this point for illustrative purposes and more in-depth analysis of other markets will follow. Suffice it to say that the lack of volume on the 16th, the penetration of the two week old value area ($23-$23 1/2) on the 17th followed by the sharp late range extension down, and the subsequent and continuous sell-off on the 18th gave ample warning that trouble was afoot. The market clearly exhibited a major selling imbalance. But unless the strictly fundamental analyst following this stock considered the probability of a dividend cut, the sell-off probably came as a surprise. Even if the news had been anticipated, the timing of the announcement was unexpected and allowed no reaction time. Those who reacted to the news by selling the delayed opening were filled on or near the lows of the day that occurred during the first hour of trade on the 19th.

We noted that the market moved lower in the Union Carbide example due to an influx of selling, an influx that created an imbalance; many impatient sellers outnumbering relatively patient buyers. The existence of this imbalance created inevitably lower prices. To futher illustrate the market's condition, we seek to sense this imbalance, discover who causes it and then study their behavior patterns. Our goal is to deduce if this net buying or selling activity can be expected to continue or if the amount that needed to be transacted has already been transacted.

# Chapter 9

# Defined Opportunities and the Types of Response

**M**arkets regularly offer the opportunity to either buy or sell at a set price to all participants. Those close to the market monitor the information that it generates, knowing that their interpretation of this market-generated information is a major portion of their decision-making process.

After ascertaining the proximity of the most recent price to value, the informed participant looks at the type of response present. For example, if the most recent transactions produced prices above value, the market's collective selling response to a price above value can be absent, thereby displaying acceptance or fairness. Or the selling response could occur as expected, and the market could fall back somewhat or all the way back to the point where the imbalance began. Or, if no response occurs after a time, the other timeframe buyers who created the buying imbalance seen at lower prices could move up and buy at the higher prices. This would indicate that buyers as a group were maintaining a very aggressive stance, initiating transactions above value. Assuming trade is being increasingly facilitated at these higher prices, the market is strong and the trend can be expected to continue up.

Determining how the market reacts after a price imbalance unfolds tells us about the condition of the market, and lets us have more information from which to draw further reasonable expectations. For example, an other timeframe buyer-motivated price imbalance causing higher prices tells us not to expect other timeframe selling to enter quickly. Now, at higher prices, does the other timeframe seller activity buffer the market, causing the market to fall back? If so, does the market fall more or less than halfway from the extreme of the recent buying imbalance? If a significant selling response occurs, one expects that the market should be contained for at least some period at those lower prices, and that the high of the day can reasonably be expected to hold at least over the next hour.

What if the other timeframe seller buffers the market only so much that the market does not fall back halfway from the extreme of recent imbalance, but only one fourth or less? What if the market hangs on or near its high, advertising for the other timeframe seller, but not receiving any selling response? The obvious conclusion is that the response that the market receives after an imbalance has created a price movement informs the participants as to how imbalanced the market is and how much further price must go to find a two-sided area of balance and equilibrium.

Another distinction to be made which illuminates the condition of the market and the type of response to be expected involves the degree of aggressiveness of the dominant other timeframe group. By identifying the presence of other timeframe buyers versus sellers by inspecting and comparing extremes, range extensions and TPO counts, we can further categorize these indicators by where they occur in relation to yesterday's value area.

**Given that one of the other timeframe groups will cause an extreme, range extension or TPO imbalance;**

**and given that the participation of the other timeframe group is voluntary and not motivated by necessity at this moment;**

**then, to the extent that one of the other timeframe groups is dominant in creating an extreme, range extension or TPO imbalance, and is participating at disadvantageous prices in reference to yesterday's value, it is displaying very aggressive and abnormal behavior, behavior likely to continue if conditions remain the same.**

In other words, if the other timeframe buyers are buying within or above yesterday's value, creating a buying extreme, a buying range extension and/or a TPO imbalance to the buy side, this is abnormal activity. This abnormal behavior indicates that other timeframe buyers as a group do not feel they have time on their side.

We label other timeframe buying activity (buying extremes, range extensions up and TPO buying) within or above yesterday's value as **initiating buying**.

We label other timeframe selling activity (selling extremes, range extensions down and TPO selling) within or below yesterday's value as **initiating selling**.

We label other timeframe buying activity (buying extremes, range extensions up and TPO buying) below yesterday's value as **responsive buying**.

We label other timeframe selling activity (selling extremes, range extensions down and TPO selling) above yesterday's value as **responsive selling**.

## Today's Market Activity _Within_ Yesterday's Value Area

```
                    ———————— Yesterday's Value Area
  ┌───────────────
  │
  ▼
 ┌─┐
 │ │        E ———————┐ Initiating Selling Extreme
 │ │        E
 │ │        DEF
 │ │        DEF                ▲
 │ │        DEF ————————————┐| Initiating Buying Range Extension
 │ │      ▲ zDEFG
 │ │   I  │ zDFG
 │ │   n  │ yzDGHI
 │ │   i  │ yzACHIJ
 │ │   t  │ yzABCIJ  ——————————
 │ │   i  │ yzABCIJK         | Initiating Selling TPO
 │ │   a  │ yABK
 │ │   l  │ yABK
 │ │        yA
 │ │   B  │ yA
 │ │   a  │ y ——————┐
 │ │   l  │ y        | Initiating Buying Extreme
 │ │      ▼ y ———————┘
 └─┘
```

## Today's Market Activity <u>Above</u> Yesterday's Value Area

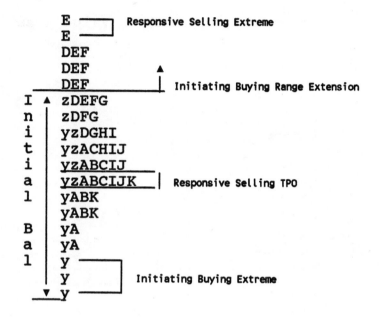

```
E ─────┐    Responsive Selling Extreme
E ─────┘
DEF
DEF              ▲
DEF ─────────────┘   Initiating Buying Range Extension
I  ▲ zDEFG
n  │ zDFG
i  │ yzDGHI
t  │ yzACHIJ
i  │ yzABCIJ
a  │ yzABCIJK │  Responsive Selling TPO
l  │ yABK
   │ yABK
B  │ yA
a  │ yA
l  │ y
   │ y ─────┐  Initiating Buying Extreme
   ▼ y ─────┘
```

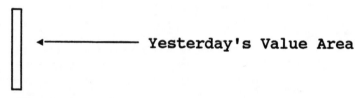

◄─────────────── Yesterday's Value Area

© 1984 CBOT

## Today's Market Activity <u>Below</u> Yesterday's Value Area

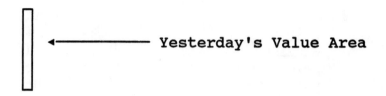

Yesterday's Value Area

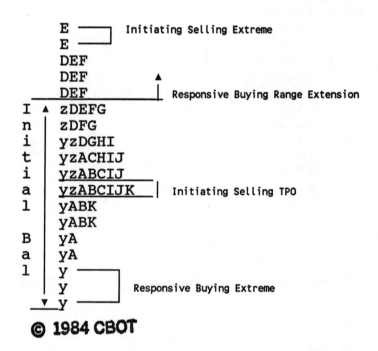

```
            E ─────┐     Initiating Selling Extreme
            E ─────┘
            DEF
            DEF            ▲
            DEF ───────────┘  Responsive Buying Range Extension
I   ▲   zDEFG
n   │   zDFG
i   │   yzDGHI
t   │   yzACHIJ
i   │   yzABCIJ
a   │   yzABCIJK  │  Initiating Selling TPO
l   │   yABK
    │   yABK
B   │   yA
a   │   yA
l   │   y ──────┐
    │   y       │  Responsive Buying Extreme
    ▼   y ──────┘
```

© 1984 CBOT

Labeling a market as predominantly initiating or responsive provides information about the speed of price change in the market. The time in which one has to act at advantageous prices can be determined as well as how directional a market can be expected to be. A preponderance of initiating activity, very abnormal and aggressive activity, usually can be seen in very fast, volatile and directional markets. Responsive activity is usually seen in slower, back and forth, relatively balanced markets.

# Chapter 10

# Organizing Data to Determine the Trend

Organizing markets with the bell curve provides insights into where the marketplace currently values the particular instrument being traded. As we shall see in a later chapter, the bell curve also reveals insights into currently highly probable day structures. This knowledge allows the individual to refine his positioning in the market beyond the reference of yesterday's value area.

But before we discuss the bell curve's other practical applications, we should confront the most important and overriding market truth that the successful participant should heed: "The trend is your friend."

How do we use the information provided thus far to determine the probable direction of the trend? We can get a reading on the probable direction and strength of the trend by organizing shorter term day bell curve information so that it displays change — imbalance — over a longer time span. In this way the participant is provided a picture of subtle imbalance occurring which will, if sustained, lead to the most attractive of trading opportunities — the trend. For example, comparing the quantity of buying extremes with the quantity of selling extremes over the past several trading sessions provides further insights into the strength or weakness of a market. The quantity and extent of buying versus selling range extensions also can be contrasted in this manner, as can TPO counts.

In order to gain a bigger picture of the market, we organize shorter term data through the tool we call the Long Term Market Activity Chart. Information extracted from a single bell curve might be akin to seeing a mosaic from up close — the individual chips of data might seem somewhat disorganized when removed from the context of longer term activity. However, information deduced from an interpretation of the Long Term Market Activity Chart might provide a bigger picture, one that we might have if we stepped back and saw the mosaic from a distance. This bigger picture is important because it often allows one to determine if sufficient imbalance exists to suggest that the market could trend directionally. The key here is that in determining whether the market can be expected to trend, we do not rely on the past movement of price, but rather on the degree of imbalance present in the market.

The Long Term Market Activity Chart is organized with price listed on the horizontal axis, the seventh column from the left. (See illustration.) Next to it is a space where the size of the value area can be indicated. On each side of this space are two groups of three columns headed "extremes, range extension and TPO count." The nearest grouping of the three to the center is labeled "initiating" and the other "responsive." The six columns to the right of the price/value area column are for buying activity, while the six on the left hand side of the page are for selling.

The Long Term Market Activity Chart is designed to illustrate the degree of imbalance

Example of Information for the Long Term Market Activity Chart:

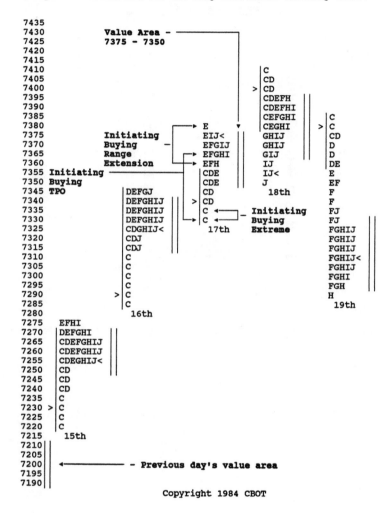

```
7435
7430            Value Area -  ──────────────┐
7425            7375 - 7350                 │
7420                                        │
7415                                        │
7410                                   │ C  │
7405                                   │ CD │
7400                                 > │ CD │
7395                                   │ CDEFH
7390                                   │ CDEFHI        ‖
7385                                   │ CEFGHI        ‖  │ C
7380            Initiating        ► E ▼ │ CEGHI      > │ C
7375            Buying             EIJ< │ GHIJ         │ CD
7370            Buying       ─     EFGIJ  ‖            │ D
7365            Range         ►    EFGHI  ‖            │ D
7360            Extension     ►    EFH    │            │ DE
7355  Initiating ─────────────────┘ CDE  │ IJ<        │ E
7350  Buying                        CDE   J           │ EF
7345  TPO          │ DEFGJ          CD      18th       │ F
7340               │ DEFGHIJ   >    CD                 │ F
7335               │ DEFGHIJ        C  ◄───── Initiating FJ
7330               │ DEFGHIJ   ►    C  ◄─────  Buying     FJ
7325               │ CDGHIJ<        17th       Extreme    FGHIJ  ‖
7320               │ CDJ                                   FGHIJ  ‖
7315               │ CDJ   ‖                               FGHIJ
7310               │ C                                     FGHIJ<
7305               │ C                                     FGHIJ
7300               │ C                                     FGHI
7295               │ C                                     FGH    ‖
7290             > │ C                                     H
7285               │ C                                       19th
7280                  16th
7275     EFHI
7270   │ DEFGHI
7265   │ CDEFGHIJ   ‖
7260   │ CDEFGHIJ
7255   │ CDEGHIJ<
7250   │ CD
7245   │ CD
7240   │ CD
7235   │ C
7230 > │ C
7225   │ C
7220   │ C
7215      15th
7210 │
7205 │
7200 │ ◄──────────── - Previous day's value area
7195 │
7190 │
```

EXAMPLE OF FILLING OUT THE LTMAC:

LONG TERM MARKET ACTIVITY CHART(C)
(C) Copyright Market Logic School 1986, All Rights Reserved

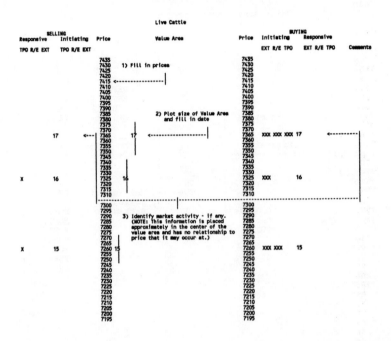

Live Cattle

apparent in the market. The preparer sorts the market activity — extremes, range extensions and the TPO count — into either initiating or responsive type activity and then plots it alongside the value area of the corresponding day that experienced that activity. Initiating activity is marked with a block to visually show its significance in creating the condition of imbalance. Responsive activity, on the other hand, is marked with an "x."

For example, note on the illustrations that when a day profile displays three forms of initiating buying activity, three dark blocks are posted as demarcations of the strong imbalanced condition. Responsive activity, since it is not as significant a contributory factor to the condition of continued imbalance, is represented on the outer columns of the chart with less visually dark demarcations.

Organizing day market activity on the Long Term Market Activity Chart allows significant insight into the current condition of the market. This is because the LTMAC so obviously displays imbalance in the market. It bears repeating that imbalance is the essence of the market; it causes a trend, the most attractive of trading opportunities. The condition of extensive imbalance doesn't self-correct quickly.

## A Few Comments on the LTMAC

There are different categories or prototypical conditions that are illustrated by the Long Term Market Activity Chart. The first category, Category One, displays an imbalanced situation, a market that can either be expected to continue trending or move sideways as the imbalance subsides somewhat, but not sharply in the direction opposite the trend. In this mode, the Chart displays a pronounced visual imbalance due to

EXAMPLE OF HOW THE MARKET CAN UNFOLD:

1) Imbalance -> 2) Balance -> 3) Test -> 4) New Imbalance

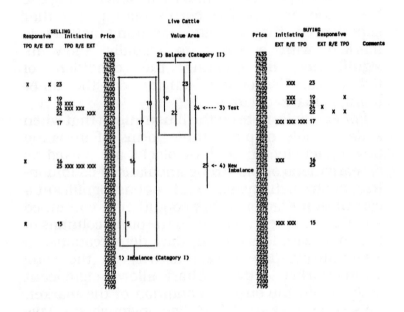

the presence of more net initiating activity (either buying or selling).

In a market that can be expected to either trend lower or hover, substantial initiating selling will be evident without correspondingly substantial initiating buying. The left side of the chart will be studded with more boxes and x's than the right, indicating greater ~~buying~~ *SELLING* than ~~selling~~ *BUYING*. Responsive buying, a less assertive mode of activity, may be evident in a Category One market. Yet the market can remain bearish, so long as larger, lower value areas indicate that the market is facilitating trade at lower prices.

Different degrees of imbalance are illustrated in the LTMAC, because one trend will behave differently from the next depending on market conditions and the maturity of the trend. On one end of the spectrum of the Category One mode will be a lazy, emerging trend, displaying a backing and filling type of activity which progressively works directionally. This type of trend in a bull phase would have higher highs, at least a two-thirds retracement to a higher low, and back up to higher highs, etc. On the other end of the spectrum is a climaxing-type trend, where volatile, one timeframe gapping movement is featured. This type of activity usually happens late in the development of the trend, particularly a mature trend, and usually precedes a turnaround.

Category Two, the second mode of the Long Term Market Activity Chart, is the balanced situation wherein the market cannot be expected to offer sustained directional movement. This has been referred to as a trading range or sideways moving market — a trendless, balanced situation — where a roughly equal proportion of initiating buying and selling and responsive buying and

selling cancel each other out. The market which is
backing and filling and exhibits the early stages of
a trend will display a great deal of Category Two-
type LTMAC behavior.

# Chapter 11

# Day Structures

**W**hen one day's transactional activity is organized into the normal distribution (or bell curve) format, several recurring and distinct prototypical patterns emerge. We refer to these patterns as **day structures**, and they serve as guideposts for anyone — hedger and speculator alike — seeking to position himself in the market. A trader who has developed the ability to identify which day structure is occurring as it unfolds is rewarded greatly, as different day structures offer dramatically different opportunities.

A strategy which incorporates the use of day structure identification is viable a high percentage of the time. This is because each day structure, while providing certain characteristic trading opportunities, shows distinct visual and behavioral characteristics, and establishes prototypical or usual range parameters. Should a prototypical day structure unfold as expected, ideal trade placement can frequently be exacted. In Chapter 8 we saw an example of one of these day structures — the trend day — in the big sell-off of Union Carbide stock on May 18. There are several other prototypical day patterns, all merely reflections of the degree of imbalance existing on the day.

### The Non-Trend Day

The non-trend day occurs when both longer timeframe buyer and seller groups are absent from the marketplace. This indicates directionless, trendless and quiet market behavior. It is a symptom of a stalling auction process, caused either through the attrition of interested participants (presumably because the price level does not motivate participation) or because of outside events such as holidays. The shape of a non-trend day is parabolic: an exceptionally tight high-low range with no pronounced selling or buying excesses present. Price movement during the trading session lacks conviction; no market imbalance, nor any tremendous anxiety to transact business can be deciphered. It is similar to the calm either before or after a storm. Depending upon its appearance within the context of recent market activity, the non-trend day's occurrence can be construed as either a harbinger of change in direction or as a rest day before a continuation of the trend.

The non-trend day is a signal that other timeframe buyers and sellers are on the sidelines, either because of lack of receptivity to the offered price level or because an outside event motivates abstinence. Outside events which could bring about a non-trend day include impending reports (trade balance, crop production, etc.) or political events (elections, State of the Union addresses, Fed chairmen testifying, etc.), or holiday doldrums (especially bank holidays in which the primary market is closed).

### The Normal Day

The normal day structure is the most common day type, appearing in either its basic form or in some variation in days of other types. The normal

NON-TREND DAY                NORMAL DAY


```
                              E
ABC                           E
ABCHIJ                        zDE
ABCEHJ                        zDEF
ABCEHJ                        zDEFG
BCDEGJ                        zCDEFG
BDEFGKL                       zCDFGH
BFKGL                         yzACDGHI
BFL                           yzACHIJ
                              yABCIJK
                              yABCIJK
                              yABK
                              yABK
                              yAB
                              yA
                              y
                              y
                              y
```

day occurs during a trending market — Category
One on the LTMAC — usually after a big directional move, when the imbalance which has
recently dominated the market is rectified and the
market "rests." It also occurs widely during a
trading range market — Category Two on the
LTMAC — which, by definition, has no single,
overpowering driving force. Since the normal day
frequently provides both buying and selling
opportunities, getting good trade location is
especially important. The characteristics which
distinguish a normal day include: a fairly wide initial balance set up by local participants as they
service orders (generally 80% or more of the day's
range is contained within the initial balance); the
presence of defined top and/or bottom extremes;
and a rotating action as the market probes from
one end of the developing value area to the other.
The market may extend beyond the initial range,
but usually this move is not robust and acts to
attract the opposite response. These probes which
meet with the opposite response — a selling probe
meets with buying that causes a buying extreme
— give the market its bell-shaped curve.

### The Normal Variation Day

The hybrid of the normal day, the normal variation day, also occurs both when the market is in a
trading range and when it is in a trend. It visually
resembles a normal day with its gentle, bell curve
shape, but the normal variation day differs in that
the market moves directionally on the day
because of an increased degree of imbalance present in the market.

The normal variation day's initial balance is
usually wider than the non-trend day's, similar to
the normal day. The wide initial balance provides
reference points that — early in the session —the
market has gone high enough to attract both buy-

ing and selling. Unlike the normal day, in which the initial balance makes up most of the day's range, the normal variation day makes a significant range extension. This range extension is usually dynamic, and can on occasion double the initial balance on a particularly active directional day. More usual is the range extension equaling the initial balance. The significant directional probing which overwhelms the early balance found in the session's first hour characterizes the normal variation day. This "overwhelming" activity indicates a greater degree of imbalance and in a trending market more often moves in the direction of the major trend.

Whether a given day will unfold as a normal day or a normal variation day depends on the dominant other timeframe participant group's degree of anxiety to enter the market. A high level of anxiety tends to spur the development of a normal variation day as aggressive buying or selling overwhelms the local trader community and other day timeframe participants who use initial extremes as references. In other words, the market opens at an area which neutralizes the shorter timeframe participant group's opinion on news and fundamental developments which have occurred since the previous session's settlement. The market then proceeds to find a fair, balanced area by probing higher and lower, servicing the orders of the other timeframe participants, and in doing so discovering price areas at which selling and buying imbalance exist. Whether the rest of the day's activity will unfold so as to produce a normal variation day or a normal day will depend on the extent to which order influx continues and the extent to which the influx is primarily interested in probing one direction only.

Different from the normal day scenario, in

## NORMAL VARIATION

```
y
y
y
yIK
yIK
yHIK
yzHIK
yzABCHIJK
yzABCDHIJK
yzABCDHJ
yzDGH
zDG
zDG
DFG
DF
DEF
DEF
EF
EF
EF
EF
E
E
E
E
```

which high prices attract selling and low prices attract buying, directional moves on the normal variation day often attract a contrary type of activity. Stated simply, the market is nervous: higher prices attract more buying; lower prices draw out more selling. This condition continues until the market reaches a new excess where traders with the opposite opinion are willing to respond to the advertised opportunity. Once the opposite activity is achieved, the market re-establishes a degree of balance at the new price levels.

### The Trend Day

The trend day is among the least common, but most dynamic, prototypical day structures. It occurs only 5% to 15% of the time, depending on the condition of the market. In a trading range or sideways moving market, the trend day cannot be expected to occur as frequently as in an emerging trend market, when open interest and outside participation are growing. The maturing trend, and particularly the topping trend markets can be expected to feature the greatest frequency of trend days.

The trend day is a climactic move in which the market is dominated and overcome by either the net buying or net selling of the other timeframe participant group.

In a trend day, price moves directionally as if on a one-way street. If the market is rallying, new highs will not attract selling, as is normal and occurs on a normal day. Rather, new highs only deliver a brief rest followed by more buying; if the market is breaking, new lows serve only to attract more selling in time. Short pauses in the directional movement are often caused by day time-frame traders (usually local pit traders) who attempt to pick tops or bottoms. Without other timeframe traders to back up those who are fading the trend day movement, these short timeframe traders win no immediate gratification for their boldness. They have no choice but to exit their positions with small profits, scratches, or losses. The action of these traders exiting their trades only serves to accentuate the prevailing market direction.

While a market that is in a typical (non-trend, normal, normal variation or neutral) day structure mode will chop back and forth across the day's trading range, a trend day moves solidly in one direction. Although small setbacks or rallies may occur, they are generally short-lived and fail to draw the opposite response and re-establish balance to the market. In contrast to the typical day — when, with good trade location, one might profitably trade both sides of the market — the trend day rewards either buyers, if a trend day up, or sellers, if a trend day down. Whether or not the buyer of a trend day up got on board early and from good early trade location is not critical on a day like this, since the trend day should close on or very near the extreme of the day.

Anxiety is perhaps the key characteristic of the trend day.Emotional despair or euphoria dominates the mindset of the market as price leads value. The other timeframe buyer or seller group overwhelms the market and, in doing so, works at full tilt. Representatives of the dominant group either have business that must be done now (hedgers); or have determined the market is ready to make a decisive move and that they must be on board (speculators); or, influenced by both motivations, they see their fraternity active and feel they must participate as well (portfolio managers).

CREEPING TREND DAY                    DOUBLE DISTRIBUTION TREND DAY

```
A                                     A
A                                     A
A                                     A
A                                     AB
AB                                    AB
B                                     BC
B                                     BCD
B                                     BCDE
B                                     BCDE
BC                                    CDE
C                                     CDEF
C                                     CDEF
C                                     CDEF
CD                                    DEF
DE                                    F
DE                                    F
DEF                                   FG
EF                                    FGH
EF                                    FGHI
F                                     FGHIJ
F                                     GHIJK
FG                                    GHIJK
GH                                    GHIJK
GH                                    GHIJKL
GH                                    GHIJKL
GHI                                   GHIJKL
HI                                    HIJKL
HI                                    HIJKL
I                                     HJKL
IJ                                    KL
IJK                                   KL
JK                                    L
KL                                    L
KL
KL
L
L
```

Trend days have definite behavioral characteristics. The market gives several cues or messages early that indicate the possibility of a trend
day unfolding. To begin with, trend days tend to
start out slowly. They rarely occur on the day of a
major government report. The market usually is
relatively quiet and the usual volatility seen in the
first hour is distinctly absent, similar to a non-
trend day. Few participants seem interested in the
market, and they fade or ignore the initial, directional range extension. As the other timeframe net
group — either the buyer or seller — takes charge
of the market, the day timeframe traders who
have faded the market hold open losses. Their
short covering or selling helps create the next
directional move.

On trend days, the market tends to open on or
near one extreme and close on or very near the
other. For example, on a trend day up, the market
should score lows early and close on or near its
highs. On a trend day down, the action is just the
converse.

Trend days take two basic forms: the creeping
trend day and the double distribution. The creeping trend day moves in relatively small, yet consistent, increments throughout the day. The market
moves, making new highs (on a trend day up) at
least every third half hour, but not with enough
velocity to discourage those who are fading the
directional movement. This type of steady march-
ing goes on all day until the market closes on or
very near its highs. It is important to note that in a
big market, the creeping trend day can be
extremely violent, particularly in the latter half of
the session. In such a case, each increment can be
expected to be more volatile. This type of day is
dangerous because the market will sometimes

NEUTRAL DAY                RUNNING PROFILE DAY

| NEUTRAL DAY | RUNNING PROFILE DAY |
|---|---|
|  | E |
| I | E |
| IJ | E |
| EIJ | E |
| DEIJ | E |
| DEIJK | DE |
| DEIJK | CDE |
| DEIJK | CDE |
| DEIJK | BCDE |
| DEFGIJK | BCDE |
| DEFGIJK | BCE |
| DEFGHIJK | ABCE |
| DEFGHIJK | ABEF |
| DEFGHJK | ABF |
| DEFGHJK | AF |
| DEFGHJK | AF |
| EGHK | F |
| GH | F |
| GH | F |
| H | FG |
|  | G |
|  | GHJ |
|  | GHIJK |
|  | GHIJKL |
|  | HIJKL |
|  | HIJKL |
|  | HIJK |
|  | IK |
|  | I |

© 1984 CBOT

overreact and reverse direction. (See running profile.)

The other common form of trend day displays a double distribution when organized by profile. The double distribution trend day is shaped like two normal days, one right on top of the other: the market creates two bell curves which are separated by a brief time-price relationship known as a **price trend**. Early in the day, the market builds value within a relatively quiet to average size high-low range. During the course of the session, however, this value area proves inadequate as an area which balances buyers and sellers. A net imbalance occurs. It is neutralized, often in a quick and violent manner. The market moves directionally, setting up a new normal profile, where the market re-establishes balance, rotates and trades much like a normal day before closing on its extreme. The double distribution trend day is frequently an exhaustion or excess day.

### The Neutral Day

The neutral day occurs in circumstances similar to those of the non-trend day, although often it appears in a more active market than the quiet surroundings which typify the non-trend day scenario. When a neutral day is ready to occur, market participants lack the conviction needed to make a long-term trade, or buyers and sellers engage in a tug-of-war over market direction.

Neutral days can often be excellent harbingers of change in direction. They frequently occur at the extremes of trading ranges or after big directional moves. Tops and bottoms of swing moves are frequently neutral days, and oftentimes several neutral days occur in a row.

In the classic and most common neutral day, the market builds a value area similar to that seen on a normal day. The difference is that on a nor-

mal day, the large initial balance established by
the local traders serves to contain the day's range;
on a neutral day, the market extends its range
both higher and lower. Generally, neither range
extension can be sustained, and the market
closes in the middle of the range, the metaphorical
tug- of-war unsettled.

Not all neutral days conclude with such an
impasse. In a rarer type of neutral day, the market
does not close in the middle of developing value,
but rallies or breaks late in the session and closes
on or near the extreme for the day. This type of
action, occurring outside of holiday markets or
otherwise abnormally quiet conditions, has a high
probability of directional continuation. Valuable
information can be gleaned from this type of
behavior. For instance, does the market score new
highs first in a lethargic manner before breaking
and settling weakly? This type of activity would
indicate that the tug-of-war has been won by the
sellers.

Assuming this activity did not occur in a holiday
market environment, lower prices might be
expected.

Quiet non-trend type days in which the market
scores a high or low by one or two ticks beyond the
initial balance must also be classified as neutral
days, but would not hold the same significance as
a neutral day that facilitated a reasonable amount
of trade. This is because whether or not the market is fulfilling its purpose of facilitating trade is
much more significant market-generated information than the fact that a slight imbalance is
occurring.

Sometimes the market forms what appears to
be a classic neutral day. However, after scoring
the first range extension fails to continue directionally, the market reverses and extends the

range in the opposite direction with gusto. This
type of neutral day generally fits in the category of
a "running profile" day.

### The Running Profile Day

Unpredictable and erratic, the running profile
day is an anomaly among the more stable day
structures with fairly recurrent parameters. It
breaks the hearts of trend followers and rewards
the brave souls willing to fade the prevailing early-
day market direction.

Running profile days generally occur when the
market is either forming a trend day structure or a
normal variation day structure. As previously discussed, under normal conditions the market
rotates, breaking to attract buyers and rallying to
give sellers their opportunity. Usually, the market
creates an excess top or bottom which accommo-
dates the orders of responsive other timeframe
traders.

On the running profile day, however, the market
tends to be moving in a one-timeframe mode. For
instance, if the market makes new highs, it will
not set back far enough to service the orders of
buyers. But at some point during the session, like
a pendulum, the market begins to reverse its
direction. After making a top or bottom, the market slowly grinds and later rushes the other way.
All the buyers or sellers who would normally
provide balance to the market upon a rotation in
the second direction are now tentative or entirely
absent. Their orders have all been filled. And the
farther the market swings without the resistance
of opposite activity, the more momentum it picks
up. A neutral day structure results from the violent price reversals endemic to the running
profile.

Running profiles, like non-trend days and neutral days, frequently occur at market tops and

bottoms. This structure is also often set in motion by an emotionally charged news event. Other than the brute directional activity of a major trend crescendo or a stock market panic, the running profile day is the most volatile type of day structure.

# Chapter 12

# How the Different Day Structures Interact

**B**eing able to correctly identify the expected day structure as it unfolds affords indispensable knowledge for trade management, and if a position is being either entered or exited, ideal trade placement can be exacted. Significantly, not only do these day structures unfold in a prototypical manner, but they interact with each other in what are understandable and often predictable day-by-day behavioral patterns.

*Non-Trend Day*

As we have already discussed, non-trend days tend to occur when the market has stagnated at a price level. The doldrums can grip the market for several days prior to a major change of trend, at the extremes of a defined trading range, or when outside events such as holidays, reports, or political events act to preclude major decision-making by market participants. The important thing to remember about non-trend days is that they signal lack of trade facilitation at the current level. The absence of trade means a major move may be imminent.

When the market has ended a major trend, it is common to see a series of non-trend days. The market has accomplished its long-term objectives,

but an opposing market opinion has not yet
surfaced to seize control of the situation. This is
reasonable, for markets generally do not perform
an abrupt about-face after a major move. The
changes that occur in a market that has finished
one trend and is not ready to start a new one are
similar to the changes in the ocean's tide. Just as
it is nearly impossible to determine which wave
marks the exact high tide point, so is it
exceptionally difficult to grasp when a market will
begin a new trend in the opposite direction.

For an example of how non-trend days can
occur in a series, consider the Soybean market in
late 1986 to early 1987.

When the bull market of 1983 came to an end,
the Bean market, like other agricultural markets,
slowly entered a long-term bear market. This
phase took considerable time to develop. The
market ground its way down for more than three
years and hit a long-term bottom in the autumn of
1986.

During this time, the Bean market slowly
emptied out. Local traders and outside
speculative interests alike abandoned this almost
nominal market for the volatile markets emerging
in bonds, currencies and stock index futures.
Open interest and volume reached low levels, as
only commercial firms interested in hedging their
inventories and pricing their needs played a major
role as outside participants.

The result of this lack of interest was a
proliferation of non-trend days. Where once the
Soybean market could trade a dollar range in a
week's time during the height of the growing
season, traders were now getting accustomed to a
ten cent high-low range. Rather than the 15 to 20
cent daily ranges seen in the previous decade, the
Soybean market labored to traverse a four cent

range. Quite simply, there was nothing going on in the market, and the volatility and day structure reflected this.

During this quiet period, non-trend days were rather common, and normal days were the most common day structure. Low volatility, relatively small high-low ranges and small value areas were the result of an absence of other timeframe activity.

Non-trend days can also be seen when the market probes the high or low end of a trading range.

As a market nears one extreme of a trading range, the ambition of other timeframe buyers or sellers frequently wanes. A portion of these traders have been positioned in the market correctly and are profitable; they now begin to close out their positions to take profits. As this occurs, few traders remain confident of continuation. This explains why markets are very volatile near tops and bottoms.

Without the large number of confident other timeframe traders to carry on the battle, the market will frequently reach the extreme of its trading range with all the signs of an impending break-out. Perhaps the market will near this extreme in a volatile, climaxing movement, often in the form of a trend day, or a normal variation day which points to continuation.

It is on the day of expected continuation at the extreme of a trading range that the market will turn in a non-trend day. This type of non-trend day is referred to as a **test day**. At this point, the market is poised to go higher or lower and is now testing the extreme. More often than not (in a trading range), the market fails the test.

Although it usually takes some time (a day or more), other market participants become aware of the vulnerability of the market at its current levels. Accordingly, they decide to fade the most recent momentum of the market. Depending on their timeframe, these traders either buy and hold, or sell and hold (if they have a long timeframe) or they probe the market by fading extremes (short timeframe). If the market does not give them gratification immediately, they look to scratch their trade.

Once the tug-of-war between other timeframe buyer and other timeframe seller ends, the market can either break out of the trading range and continue in the direction of the most recent dominant group, or it can begin the journey back across the width of the entire trading range.

The non-trend day will also make its appearance when a market is open during a major holiday or before a major report or political event. Let's review each case briefly.

In a market such as the bond market, the role of investment and commercial banks is crucial. These institutions represent much of the commercial interest in such a market. On a holiday in which banks close and major traders are out of the office, it would stand to reason that these clients would not be very active. For this reason, local traders at a futures exchange would find themselves with plenty of time on their hands and little trade. The foreign currency markets face a similar situation. They are dominated by international banks and a few very active corporations. If Japanese businesses are closed for a national holiday, it follows that there will not usually be an active session in the Japanese yen. The end result on such a day is often a non-trend profile.

Market participants gain much of their information from a wide variety of reports released by the government. In financial markets, participants must pay attention to Gross National Product reports, unemployment statistics, trade balance figures, and a host of other facts and figures released by the Commerce Department on a regular basis. Physical commodity futures markets, too, are subject to the release of government data, weather forecasts, etc. Here, the United States Department of Agriculture (USDA) issues a plethora of reports detailing everything from gross planting intentions to weather forecasts to estimated harvests. Participants use these figures to help shape their current market perspective. As a consequence, only those traders with a long timeframe and strong conviction will carry their positions through a report. Because these traders have probably already established their positions at more attractive levels, they have nothing to do on the eve of a report.

It also stands to reason that markets would remain quiet before important political events. Take a presidential speech, for example. If there are tensions between the United States and the Soviet Union, grain traders will tend to even their positions before the President speaks. They know from past experience that an address to the nation can entail anything from the announcement of a summit to iron out differences to a total embargo on grain shipments. Similarly, bond traders will tend to stand aside before an administration submits its version of the federal budget to Congress. The budget, as these traders know, can contain many surprises, from deficits to surpluses.

The key to understanding the non-trend day is to recognize that the other timeframe trader, the market participant who drives the market, is absent or extremely quiet. This type of trader stays away from the market because he sees no opportunity at the current price level or because he awaits a report or the outcome of a political event. Without the participation of the other timeframe trader, the market does not stand the chance of facilitating trade.

And because we know the chief function of the market is to facilitate trade, price will have to move directionally to arouse the interest of the other timeframe trader.

### Neutral Days

Like non-trend days, neutral days are often good indicators of an impending change in market direction at the end of a trend, on trading range extremes and during holiday trading. Unlike the non-trend day, the neutral day tends to be more volatile, as long timeframe traders are present, even if not acting out of strong conviction. As far as its meaning for continuation or change goes, a neutral day that lacks this volatility is basically interchangeable with a non-trend day.

As we discussed earlier, the distinguishing component of a standard neutral day is range extension on both sides of the initial balance. A neutral day's range extensions can be slight or can be significantly in excess of the 20% of initial balance parameter that defined the normal day. When backed by no strong convictions, these range extensions tend to fizzle out, causing the market to close somewhere in the middle of the day's range. At times, however, the market can reject one of these range extensions before closing in the opposite direction in a dynamic fashion. When this happens, the day is classified as a running profile day structure.

Neutral days frequently come at the end of a major directional move, often forming and signaling a top or bottom of a swing in the market. Generally, this extreme follows several days of initiating activity which serve to climax the trend. That group of traders with the advantage — meaning price movement in their favor — pushes its opposite up against a wall. Typically, those traders who have the opposite opinion on the market back away from trading. Swing traders who look for three to five day moves will only probe the market if they receive good trade location. Longer term traders will take a passive approach, responding to attractive prices far from the prevailing value in the marketplace.

Given this scenario — in which one group of traders has everything in its favor while its counterparts are throwing in the towel — the market tends to act to shut off the current imbalance. In other words, if a given market is rallying and more and more buyers forge ahead as weak sellers retreat, the market will tend to achieve prices that will first attract responsive selling activity and then dampen the enthusiasm of even the most ardent buyers.

When this situation occurs, the market is ripe for a neutral day. As the potential neutral day unfolds, initiating traders retain control of the market. However, the participants holding positions at prevailing price levels are thinning their ranks as some traders take profits and others are scared off by the extreme level of the market (this second group prefers to wait for a setback or rally before entering the market). Now the market has gone far enough to attract the responsive trader. Rallies begin to be met by resting sell orders, and breaks find buy orders below the market. Once the responsive trader meets the initiating trader head to head, the market has the potential to regain balance and possibly develop a new imbalance in the opposite direction.

The neutral day in these circumstances is frequently referred to as a blow-off top or bottom. As the market moves into responsive territory (i.e., range extension up or down), the other timeframe trader is now actively fading the directional move of the market. His orders contain the market because they will not be closed out at the end of the day's trading. Faced with this type of challenge, short term initiating traders are forced to take losses, as their trades do not give them gratification. This activity, in turn, attracts additional pressure from swing traders who are beginning to see some results from their efforts. As the market begins to reject its extreme, the level of anxiety among both groups of traders begins to heighten. Initiating traders want to take profits or cut short their losses, and responsive traders sense that a potential change in direction is imminent. The net result of this activity is either a break or rally which results in a range extension in the opposite direction. This move should act to attract one last wave of initiating traders who do not want to miss what they perceive to be a buying or selling opportunity. This activity serves to drive the market back into its value area by the close.

This type of neutral day can be described by likening market participants to passengers on a boat who rush to the starboard side to look at an interesting sight. Once the balance of the boat is destroyed, they become frightened and rush to the port side, hoping to rectify the situation. Instead, their panic only serves to tilt the vessel in the opposite direction. It is only when the passengers regroup in the middle of the deck that the balance is restored.

## Normal and Normal Variation Days

The normal day is the most common type of day structure. It is distinguished by the wide balance it establishes in the first hour of trading. Although the normal variation day features an initial balance which, while not necessarily smaller in absolute terms, is a smaller percentage of the daily high-low range than the normal day, both day structures tend to trade back and forth in a choppy manner, forming a bell curve. The oscillating trade serves to provide both buyers and sellers with several opportunities to enter the market. Although the normal day can produce a range extension, the market lacks follow-through. The range extension acts to widen the developing value area.

As the most common type of day structure, the normal day occurs in all market conditions. It is seen when a market is consolidating at a top or bottom, within trading ranges, and also during trends.

Near the end of a trend, particularly when a market is forming a long-term bottom, the normal day makes frequent appearances. These normal days are somewhat compact compared with their ranges at higher levels, due to the lack of volatility at the bottoming levels. Still, despite the lack of interest shown by speculative other timeframe traders at market bottoms, there is some level of business that must be done. Commercial hedgers, such as grain firms that need to price soybeans or financial institutions that need to offset positions in the cash securities market, continue to trade. These hedgers seek a fair price at which to conduct their business. Understanding the market, they are willing to give the local trader an edge to encourage him to accommodate their orders.

Normal and normal variation days also occur regularly in trading ranges, sideways moving patterns which make up the vast majority of time spent trading. (When viewed over the course of a three to five year vantage point, the average market spends perhaps no more than 30% of the time in a discernible trend.) When markets reject one extreme of a trading range (frequently signaled by the presence of a neutral or non-trend day), they frequently accelerate for a short period of time, as one group of other timeframe traders exerts its power over the market. The market in a trading range is, by definition, fairly stable. Participants lack a sense of urgency. The absence of anxiety among other timeframe traders results in a market that is characterized by many days in a row of unchanged values. Although the market has made a top or bottom — and in doing so has alerted traders to impending change — longer timeframe participants know they have time to get in at favorable price levels.

When a market comes off the top or bottom of a trading range, day timeframe and shorter other timeframe traders, such as swing traders, enter the market early along with responsive, longer other timeframe traders. The result is generally a volatile session or two when it appears the market is going to make a substantial move. This move cannot be sustained for long, however, because swing traders take profits, and the key participants, the longer other timeframe traders, do not reach for the market. Indeed, the characteristic of the emerging trend is a back and forth movement of values (in a bull market, for example, a zigzagging higher high, higher low) caused by the fact that the other timeframe trader, rather than reaching for or chasing price, fades the move, thereby containing it.

Normal days in trending markets are usually rest days which serve to allow consolidation. On the other hand, the behavior of normal variation days often gives early confirmation to the beginnings of a trend. For example, in a trending market, normal variation days exhibit more range extensions in the direction of the trend than counter-trend. Furthermore, the stronger range extensions will usually point in the direction of the trend. Thus, normal variation range extensions moving against the trend will usually be weaker.

*Trend Days*

Trend days, while usually proceeding in the direction of the general trend in a trending market, can as easily move counter to the trend. When this occurs, being positioned with the trend day against the trend, even for a day trade, is not as high percentage a trade as the trend day moving in the direction of the trend. This is because one type of the rare running profile day results from a trend day that fails. Failed trend days usually develop out of counter-trend trend days, and also occur from trend days in sideways moving markets. A trend day positioned in the direction of the trend will almost always be of a greater directional magnitude than that which is counter-trend, unless the counter-trend trend day is occurring in a mature market with especially high open interest. In this case, the market, needing to be cleansed of the so-called "weak hands" riding the trend, will often move very violently in a trend day fashion, but will recover within a few days and resume the general trend.

Trend days do not tend to occur two successive days in a row, but are often followed by at least one and usually several normal or quiet normal variation days. Except in a liquidating bear or climaxing bull mode, the trend day is at least an interim climax, usually signaling the market's need to rest and regroup via one or a series of normal or normal variation days. Often, a number of rest days which follow a trend day become progressively quieter until the trend can again kick in in a robust fashion, a large normal variation day or another trend day.

One caveat must be introduced before leaving the subject of day structures. The markets have evolved to the point where in certain instruments today, legitimate, deep markets are made virtually 24 hours a day. Such is the case in the interbank market, where active currency trade takes place in Asian, European and U.S. time zones. This fact obviously changes the behavior of the market, since, for example, there is not the forcing point of a market's close with which to motivate the trader to act. Thus, examining the day structure of only one time zone does not provide the full picture, and indeed distorts the percentage of recurring prototypical day structures that would otherwise occur. Where the volume of transactions is spreading semi-equally across several time zones, activity across those time zones can be examined in order to deduce a logical pattern of trade. For example, in all U.S. time zone futures and options markets, except for foreign currencies traded at the International Monetary Market and the Philadelphia Stock Exchange, and the precious metals traded at the COMEX, neutral day structures are very infrequent. Yet in the above mentioned markets, neutral days are not at all uncommon. When viewed from the context of whether or not the IMM's range extension is indeed a range extension from price levels seen in the Far East and London, another picture altogether is seen. This is not to say that the concept of recurring prototypical day structures becomes obsolete once a market becomes intercontinental, but rather that adjustments must be made for this fact.

The structure of the world's capital markets has been evolving rapidly and the location of the primary markets in many of the world's key assets has shifted over the past 20 years. This is another trend that can be expected to continue. With this evolution, the behavior of the markets, and specifically the character and percentage frequency of the outlined day structures cannot be expected to remain unchanged. However, by organizing activity using the tools described within this book, the participant will be able to capture, define and analyze any and all changes that take place.

# SECTION THREE:

# Decision-Making with Market-Generated Information: Interpreting Reference Points

This section will introduce a framework for a decision-making process structured around an understanding of the principles of market operation introduced in Section One and illustrated through two methods of market organization — the bell curve and the Long Term Market Activity Chart — presented in Section Two.

# Chapter 13

# An Overview of Decision-Making in the Financial Markets

The universality of all markets has been explored, and we have considered the operational truths which apply to all markets, organized financial and unorganized everyday markets alike. Numerous tools have been introduced which allow the participant to understand current conditions. Current conditions are then compared to what would be normal conditions given a particular outlook or expectations. The reader of this book, given some time to view the markets, should gain a solid foundation in how emerging, maturing and climaxed bull and bear markets differ from one another as seen through profiles (extremes, range extensions and TPO counts), expected percentage of day structure occurrence, daily and weekly high-low-close, and long-term market activity chart formations. With ability, some practical experience and these tools, measuring imbalance and thereby understanding a market's current mode becomes not only possible but quite attainable.

The reader is now ready to begin assimilating market-generated information into a structured decision-making process. This is a lifelong challenge, not one that can be learned from reading and rereading a book. Indeed, previous to the development of the curriculum offered by the Market Logic School, the financial market participant was the only professional who did not have access to a curriculum that taught formal decision-making parameters. If a professional is compensated because of his ability to interpret important data which are unintelligible to the unschooled, then the financial market participant has, until recently, been severely disadvantaged. He had only "gut instinct," "feel," or intuition, in sharp contrast to the learning process of other well-compensated professionals such as lawyers, accountants, scientists, medical professionals and the many others who deal with data interpretation and decision-making management in an environment of uncertainty.

But what must become "experiential knowledge" nevertheless can be introduced and, with sufficient reinforcement provided by the empirical experience gained from monitoring live markets, decision-making abilities can be learned and enhanced.

The challenge of successfully competing in financial markets is not unlike doing so in any other business environment. The difference for the trader is that analytical decision-making is the entire emphasis; there is nothing else to fall back on. In other businesses, personnel, successful marketing, a monopoly position, inept competition or superior service can mitigate poor buy-sell decisions, whereas in trading they do not exist. Trading, then, is a concentrated form of do-or-die analytical decision-making. The trader's mandate is to structure all entries, timing, management and exits around his knowledge of current conditions and the likelihood of change. He may ask himself:

> Is the market in a trend? If so, is it a young and emerging trend that can be expected to continue?
>
> Or, is the trend strong, mature, volatile and looking to top? Or, has the trend possibly climaxed, indicating that a break or at least a sideways movement is imminent?
>
> ...or...
>
> Is the market in a sideways movement, a trading range? If so, can that be expected to continue or is the market displaying signs of potential imbalance?

Obviously, to answer these critical questions, questions which indicate how much time the participant has to remain positioned either long or short with the odds in favor of the market not making an adverse move, intensive scrutiny and ongoing monitoring of the market are required.

The successful trader knows that the ideal position has an infinite number of fallbacks. There are times, for instance, when the market is so undervalued that the long side of a trade may be good for the day, should be good for the week, and almost certainly good for the month and year, etc. This approach stresses the importance of having time on your side. Identifying change in its early stages leads to startlingly low risk opportunities for this simple reason.

# Chapter 14

# Market Activity Nuances and Subtleties

In a preceding chapter, several prototypical day structures were introduced. By observing their recurrent behavioral characteristics we are able to reasonably project the range parameters on a daily basis. In this chapter we will make a slightly broader assessment of the data in order to identify longer term market changes in their formative or early stages. This is especially challenging, because early changes are slight and subtle, and imbalance as it is beginning is barely perceptible. Note that identifying changes early is stressed because being early offers the lowest risk opportunities.

As discussed previously, one indicator of the other timeframe participant's presence can be detected through the imbalance that creates a single print TPO buying or selling extreme. The existence of a buying extreme, for instance, indicates that sufficiently increased competition to buy has occurred at the lower levels where the single print TPOs occurred. This buying extreme creates the reference point, a benchmark that tells participants that the market has, for the time being, gone low enough to find an imbalance of buyers to sellers. The participant gains the confidence needed to aggressively buy, and the market rallies, again probing for selling activity.

An initiating buying extreme is one whose low tick is either within or above the previous day's value area, at somewhat disadvantageous prices relative to the previous day's activity.

However, this is not to say that all extremes are alike, or that the market draws an identical level of confidence from all locations where a single print extreme exists. Initiating buying extremes have already been differentiated from responsive selling extremes. But beyond this, there are further, finer categories of extremes, each caused by varying degrees of anxiousness. They give the market vastly different signals as references; participants interpret them and react with differing levels of confidence and anxiousness. Remember, it is anxiousness that causes imbalance, and continued imbalance causes the market to trend.

## Types of Extremes

### The Early Entry Extreme

The early entry extreme is the product of a highly anxious degree of net buying or net selling. As the name suggests, both the anxiousness on the part of the dominant other timeframe group, and the extreme being created are established from the opening bell. The market opens and immediately moves directionally, so that the opening price (or within a tick) ends up being the high or low price for the day. In other words, the opening creates the market's high on an early entry selling extreme, its low on an early entry buying extreme. When the market opens, the net other timeframe group that is dominant moves the market directionally, causing the extreme.

The significance of an early entry extreme lies in the observable demonstration of anxiety in the market which oftentimes indicates directional

|                        |                          |
| ---------------------- | ------------------------ |
| NORMAL EXTREME         | "NO ACTIVITY" EXTREME    |

| NORMAL EXTREME | "NO ACTIVITY" EXTREME |
| -------------- | --------------------- |
| D              | A                     |
| D              | A                     |
| D              | A                     |
| D              | ABCEFHK               |
| CDE            | ABCDFGHIJKL           |
| CDEI           | BCDFGIJKL             |
| CDEGHI         | CDGK                  |
| BCDEFGHIL      |                       |
| BCEFGHIL       | © 1984 CBOT           |
| BCFGHIL        |                       |
| ABCFGHIKL      |                       |
| ABCFGIKL       |                       |
| ABCIJK         |                       |
| ABIJK          |                       |
| ABIJK          |                       |
| ABJ            |                       |
| A              |                       |
| A              |                       |
| A              |                       |

continuation, both for the day (i.e., normal variation or a large trend day) and over the longer term. Thus, days in which the market immediately finds an imbalance and the resulting directional movement which temporarily neutralizes it are often big directional days: normal variation or aberrational (in that the initial balance is abnormally large) trend days. As well, this activity usually indicates that the other timeframe group is most dominant, and may continue to create the imbalance that will determine the trend.

The early entry extreme is not at all common in quiet, two-timeframe trading range markets. It is found more frequently in volatile, trending markets, particularly in maturing or climaxed states.

### The Normal Extreme

The normal extreme can occur at any point during the day, and is not as reliable an indication of short or long-term continuation as the early entry extreme. Nevertheless, it is caused by competition — an imbalance — and as such provides a temporary reference point as to the location of an excess. That excess may hold or it may not, but regardless, we can exact market-generated information as to the location of current resistance and/or support. A selling extreme tells us that the high may be in for the day.

### The "No Activity" Extreme

A normal extreme occurs when the dominant other timeframe group, eager to transact at a given level, creates an imbalance that causes a bounce or a rejected upside probe. But when the market is quiet, even though technically a visual extreme may be present, competition and imbalance are not all that apparent. The "no activity" extreme is not as significant as the normal or early entry types because the market is quiet and not facilitating trade. A good rule of thumb is this: when a market is not facilitating trade, discount the importance of any extremes, range extensions and TPO imbalances.

## Types of Range Extensions

Having discussed the subtle differences of extreme formation, let us now turn to range extensions and consider how two key factors influence the meaning and importance we attach to them.

Range extensions differ from one another first by the speed with which they are made. If a range extension is created by aggressive other timeframe participants, the greater the imbalance, the greater the level of aggressiveness. We presume that more passive behavior cannot be expected to continue over time, while the more aggressive behavior can be expected to continue. In other words, if one initial range extension up moves 25% beyond the initial balance while another moves up only 10%, we would conclude that the first market shows a greater degree of imbalance and is probably stronger. We would expect that the net other timeframe buying which entered, causing the more explosive range extension, will continue at best, and at least can be expected to buffer the market from falling.

Range extensions also differ from one another from the standpoint of the time at which they occur, relative to their opening. Aggressive activity can occur early or late in the day. We have found that early range extensions offer the most reliable benchmarks. As a rule, the early entry extreme is a very reliable benchmark indicating range containment as well as the probable direction of

| EARLY RANGE EXTENSION | LATE RANGE EXTENSION |
|---|---|
| A | AE |
| A | ABCE |
| A | ABCDE |
| AB | ABCDEFGH |
| AB | ABCDEFGHKL |
| AB | ABDFGHIJKL |
| AB | AFGHIJKL |
| BC | JKL |
| BC | JK |
| C | JK |
| CD | J |
| CD | |
| CD | © 1984 CBOT |
| DE | |
| DEFG | |
| EFGHI | |
| FGHIJKL | |
| FIJKL | |
| JKL | |
| JKL | |
| K | |
| K | |

the dominant other timeframe group. Likewise, a range extension that occurs early in the trading session is more significant in its reliability. An early range extension is defined as having occurred during the first 45 minutes after the initial balance. This early range extension indicates a pronounced imbalance that is more likely to continue than one which occurs later. Any range extension that occurs after this 45 minute period, while still indicating imbalance, does not indicate as strong an imbalance.

# Chapter 15

# Technical Analysis and Market Logic

The past 20 years, with the advent of telecommunications and computer technology, have seen numerous analytical methods that have gained widespread acceptance in the trading community. These methods, grouped under the general classification of "technical analysis," have become the most commonly used tools for market evaluation. For many traders, competing in the organized markets would be impossible without them.

Given that traditional forms of technical analysis are the futures industry's standard approach to market forecasting, the question arises: how does technical analysis relate to the precepts upon which Market Logic is based? Furthermore, can the Market Logician employ the basic elements of technical analysis in his decision-making parameters?

*Pluses and Minuses of Technical Analysis*

Loosely defined, technical analysis interprets — mathematically, statistically, or visually — market behavior in order to forecast the future direction of price movement. Technicians assume that markets trend and that there are specific discernible, recurrent patterns at work in the marketplace which determine price action, and display the trend. By manipulating price data into a usable format (usually open-high-low-close bars) the analyst can forecast with better than fifty percent accuracy where prices are headed in the near future.

Prior to the publication of *Markets and Market Logic*, traditional technical analysis (which includes Elliot Wave, Fibonacci, Gann analysis and cycle work) was the only objective means available by which price behavior could be evaluated and assessed. Given this, it's not unusual then that the vast majority of traders have at some point employed some variation of technical analysis in their decision-making process. While technical methods can at times be effective trading tools, these means of analysis often have drawbacks.

### 1. Technical analysis fails to take into account trade facilitation as a market condition.

Most technical indicators weigh present price behavior against that of the past. The emphasis is mostly on price behavior. Little or no attention is paid to whether the marketplace is fulfilling its purpose — to facilitate trade — at a given price level. As a result, technical indicators often misinterpret higher or lower prices as a sign of strength or weakness, when in reality directional price movement will in time be rejected by the market due to a lack of facilitation at those levels. In other words, in a bull market, lower prices with less trade facilitation create a condition that often will give the experienced trader, schooled in the principles of Market Logic, insight that a buying opportunity may be present. On the other hand, many technical models, seeing the same market behavior, would interpret the lower prices as market weakness and a selling rather than a buying opportunity.

**2. Technical analysis often becomes too "mechanical," failing to account for the character of the market (i.e., trend vs. trading range, and, if a trend, its primary direction and strength).**

Since many technical indicators (moving averages, relative strength index, stochastics, etc.) are derived through mathematical formulas, many traders delegate the task of determining market perspective to a black box. By relying too heavily on a "system," technical traders frequently fall out of touch with the ebb and flow of the markets and, should the system go astray, they have difficulty determining what current market conditions portend. This undermines the trader's confidence in his approach, and removes the most important orientation that the trader requires: whether, given current conditions, the trader feels more comfortable playing the long or the short side of the market.

Despite problems with their practical application, technical indicators do provide many advantages to traders.

**1. Technical analysis allows visualization of market activity.**

Since technical indicators are most frequently displayed graphically, traders are given an opportunity to visually relate price activity as it is occurring in the marketplace. The sole purpose of charting analysis, for instance, is to draw conclusions based on visual depictions of day-to-day price movement. Surely, a picture is worth a thousand words, particularly when presenting information vital to decision-making. (Technical analysis is not, however, the best picture, as we will see.)

## 2. Technical analysis focuses on price action not clouded by fundamental and news-related complications.

As we all have seen, a good fundamentalist can build both a bullish case and a bearish case with a similar set of supply and demand statistics. The final conclusion of any fundamental analysis must therefore be quite subjective, weighting certain circumstances while ignoring or at least downplaying others.

Rather than approaching the markets purely from a subjective position, the technical trader is forced to focus his attention on what is taking place within the marketplace. Viewed from whatever timeframe, an overbought situation is a quantitative event. To the technician, fundamental factors do exist, but their impact is already reflected in the technical data.

It is true that most technical trading methods are not sufficiently comprehensive to produce consistent results over a large sample size. Some, such as moving averages, are geared toward trending markets and "hold and pyramid" strategies while others, such as stochastics and the relative strength index, are geared toward trading range markets. There are, however, elements of many technical concepts which, when employed as a supplement to logical market analysis, add support and bring perspective to the decision-making process. What follows is an assessment of the merits of these methods and a review of how these concepts can be effectively used by the Market Logician.

### Charting

Charting is certainly unrivaled for gathering a mental picture of where market prices have been and where they appear to be going. As most

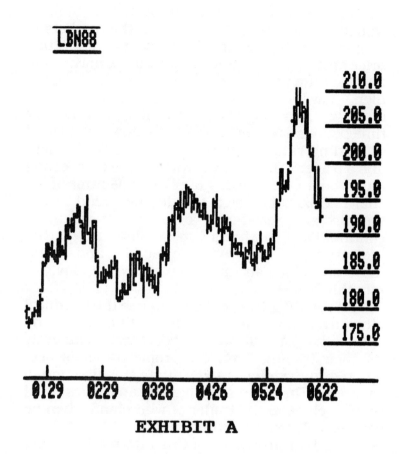

EXHIBIT A

traders are aware, price action in the markets is most commonly depicted on charts by plotting price on a vertical axis and time on the horizontal. For each time period (day, week, month, etc.), the high, low, opening, and closing prices are displayed as a "bar." When a sufficient number of time periods are displayed on the chart, the trend or trading range pattern becomes quite evident and a trader can quickly see where the market has found buying and selling over the timeframe of the chart. Chartists seek to identify trend lines, support and resistance areas, and reversal or continuation patterns in order to gather indications of future price action and trend movement (on an intraday, daily, weekly, or monthly basis).

How should a Market Logician use the technical data available from charts? Although many traders have relied on charts almost exclusively for their trading data, the profile trader is best advised to use charts to evaluate the direction of the trend. That is to say, charting analysis should provide clues to the trader of where and when he can possibly expect certain market activity to take place and, on the basis of this information, what type of market-generated information he should be looking for which will confirm or deny his suspicions. To best explain the use of charting analysis, refer to Figure A.

Figure A is a daily bar chart of price action in July 1988 Lumber. Lumber had been in an uptrend since late 1987, with prices continuing to climb into the first quarter of 1988. In late January, Lumber ended a bull market pullback by bottoming at the 178.00 level. After climbing sharply to the 195.00 mark, the market then pulled back in March to form a base at the 182.00 level. By connecting the intraday lows made at the bottoms in January and March, a trend line is formed which depicts the upward bias of the market. Coming off the lows in late March, Lumber again rallied to new highs by April. Following this move, the market once again began a pullback movement.

Consider the decision-making parameters of the chartist who had been observing the activity in Lumber and was looking for a low risk place to establish a long position. Having plotted the trend line depicted on the chart, the chartist might assume that the selloff in Lumber would continue until intraday prices intersected the trend line (or that the trend line would offer support). As prices moved still lower in May, the chartist would begin to watch the market action carefully, given that charting analysis suggests that Lumber should hold prices above the trend line. Notice for a moment what information the charting analysis has provided. In no way does the chart clearly indicate at what price to buy. It only posits that the market may hold the trend line. The chartist would therefore be watching closely for market-generated information which would indicate an aggressive other timeframe buyer, the factor that would cause a turnaround.

In essence, the chart acts as a rough outline, giving a general picture of where the market has been and allowing one to deduce possible locations where strong buying might appear. Once one has a rough idea of where turning points may develop, analysis of profiles and volume data can pinpoint if indeed such a turnaround is evident.

Examine May 9 on the chart. A chartist might be on the lookout for a possible bottom being formed in lumber and he would begin to carefully study the daily profiles (see Exhibit B). On May 9 and 10, the market displayed signs of continuing the

| | MAY 9 | MAY 10 | MAY 11 | MAY 12 | MAY 13 | MAY 16 |
|---|---|---|---|---|---|---|
| 190.4 | | | | | | |
| 190.3 | | | | | | |
| 190.2 | | | | | | |
| 190.1 | | | | | | |
| 190.0 | | | | | | |
| 189.9 | | | | | | |
| 189.8 | | | | | | |
| 189.7 | | | **JULY** | | | |
| 189.6 | | | **LUMBER** | | | |
| 189.5 | | | | | | |
| 189.5 | | | | | | |
| 189.4 | | | | | | |
| 189.3 | | | | | | |
| 189.2 | | | | | | C |
| 189.1 | | | | | | C |
| 189.0 | | | | | C | C |
| 188.9 | | C | | | C | C |
| 188.8 | DE | C | | | CI | CD |
| 188.7 | D | C | | | CEHI | CD |
| 188.6 | DE | C | | | CE | CD |
| 188.5 | DE | C | | | CEHK | CD |
| 188.4 | CDE | C | | | CDEFHK | CDE |
| 188.3 | CEFH | CD | | | CDEFGHIQ | DEFGH |
| 188.2 | CEFH | CDE | | I | CDEFGHK | DEFGHI |
| 188.1 | CDGFHIJK | CDEGH | | I | DFK | EFGHI |
| 188.0 | CGHIJK | DEFGHI | | HI | CDFGHIJK | EFHI |
| 187.9 | CGHJK | DEFGHI | | HI | DGHJK | EJ |
| 187.8 | GKQ | DEFGIJ | | HI | CDHIJK | EHIJ |
| 187.7 | K | DEHIJ | C | HI | IK | EIJ |
| 187.6 | C | DEHIJK | C | HI | IJK | EIJ |
| 187.5 | | DEIJKQ | C | GHIJ | IJ | EIJ |
| 187.4 | | DJK | C | GHJ | IJ | J |
| 187.3 | | DK | C | GHIJK | I | J |
| 187.2 | | | C | GHIJK | | J |
| 187.1 | | | C | GH | | J |
| 187.0 | | | C | DGHK | | JK |
| 186.9 | | | C | DEFGHK | | JK |
| 186.8 | | | CD | DEFGHKQ | | JK |
| 186.7 | | | CD | DEFG | | K |
| 186.6 | | | CD | DEFG | | Q |
| 186.5 | | | CD | DEFG | | K |
| 186.4 | | | CD | DE | | K |
| 186.3 | | | DEF | CD | | |
| 186.2 | | | DEFGJ | CD | | |
| 186.1 | | | DEGIJ | CD | | |
| 186.0 | | | | C | | |

| MAY 17 | MAY 18 | MAY 19 | MAY 20 | MAY 23 | MAY 24 | |
|---|---|---|---|---|---|---|
| | | C | | | | 190.4 |
| | | C | | | | 190.3 |
| | | CD | | | | 190.2 |
| | | CD | | | | 190.1 |
| | | CDJ | | | | 190.0 |
| | | CDIJ | | | | 189.9 |
| | | CDIJ | | | | 189.8 |
| | | CDEGIJ | | | | 189.7 |
| | | CDEGIJ | | | | 189.6 |
| | | CDEGIJ | | | | 189.5 |
| | | CEFG | | | | 189.5 |
| | | CEFGHIJ | | | | 189.4 |
| | | CEGHI | | | | 189.3 |
| | | EFGHJ | | | | 189.2 |
| | | CEFGHK | | | | 189.1 |
| | | CEFGK | | | | 189.0 |
| | | CEFK | | | | 188.9 |
| | | EK | | | EF | 188.8 |
| | | K | | | EF | 188.7 |
| | | K | | | EF | 188.6 |
| | K | Q | C | | CEFG | 188.5 |
| | K | | C | | CEFG | 188.4 |
| | KQ | | C | | CFGJ | 188.3 |
| | DK | | CH | | CDGHJK | 188.2 |
| | K | | CHIJ | | CHQ | 188.1 |
| | DK | | CHIJ | | CDHIJK | 188.0 |
| | D | | CFGHJK | | CDIJ | 187.9 |
| | DIK | | CDEFGIJK | CEG | CDIJ | 187.8 |
| | DIJK | | CDEFIJKP | CEGHI | CI | 187.7 |
| I | DJK | | CDEIJK | CEFGHI | C | 187.6 |
| IJ | DEFIJ | | CEIK | CDEFGHI | C | 187.5 |
| HIJ | CDEFIJ | | CEIJK | CDIJ | C | 187.4 |
| HJ | EFIJ | | CE | CDFHI | C | 187.3 |
| HJ | CFHIJ | | CIJ | CDEFJK | | 187.2 |
| FHIJ | CF | | IJ | CDFJ | | 187.1 |
| FIJ | CGHI | | IJ | CDJK | | 187.0 |
| CDFHIJK | CHI | | IJ | DJQ | | 186.9 |
| CDGHIJK | CGH | | IJ | DJK | | 186.8 |
| CDFGHIJKQ | C | | | K | | 186.7 |
| CDGJ | C | | | | | 186.6 |
| CDEFG | C | | | | | 186.5 |
| CDEFG | C | | | | | 186.4 |
| DEF | | | | | | 186.3 |
| C | | | | | | 186.2 |
| C | | | | | | 186.1 |
| C | | | | | | 186.0 |

**EXHIBIT B**

decline. Mostly present were signs of selling with
only one form of buying (on the 9th). On May 11,
the market experienced a normal day with a range
extension down, a strong initiating selling extreme
and initiating TPO selling. While the market
penetrated the 186.00 level on this day, there were
certainly no indications that the market was
attempting to bottom. On May 12, the market
displayed its first signs of other timeframe buyer
entry. Opening on its lows, Lumber rallied profile
like that of a trend day. On May 13, the market
opened still higher, but the opening half hour
proved to be the high as sellers took control of the
day. In retrospect, it is possible to say that the
rally of the 12th (which continued into the opening
of the 13th) was primarily a short-covering event.
Although some other timeframe buyers did enter
and aid in the effort, higher prices failed to
facilitate trade and consequently, the rally fizzled
late on the 16th.

On May 17, bulls were once again encouraged
as, after again opening on its lows (at 186.00),
lumber showed signs of strong responsive buying
(two forms for the day). Bulls had even more to
cheer about as the opening prices touched the
uptrend line and were greeted by a wave of buying.
However, the rally which was spurred by this
responsive buying (on the 17th, 18th and 19th)
also ran out of steam in only two days as the
market made a poor showing on the 19th. On May
20, the market opened and began selling from the
bell. However, after extending the range down in I
period, Lumber stabilized during J period and
subsequently rallied to close in the middle of
value. Though encouraged by this activity,
certainly the bulls were cautious, given that the
last two attempts to rally had failed. However, it
was becoming apparent at this time that each

time the market tried to trade through the 186.00 area, it was being met with significant imbalance, namely responsive buying. This fact should not have been surprising considering that the bar chart trend line indicated support at the 186.00 range.

On May 23, Lumber posted the lowest TPO volume of the previous two weeks. Although there was range extension, it was only by one tick, and came late in the day during K period. The move failed to follow through. The day was a quiet day and it was clear that trade was not being facilitated at this price level. To the observer of market-generated information, this fact should have been an early signal that the market had the potential to change. The presence of strong responsive buying (at levels which the start had shown should hold) in addition to the non-facilitating action of the 23rd, should have provided adequate warning. On the 24th, Lumber traded to significantly higher levels and ultimately reached 210.00 in the next two weeks.

Here was a technical analysis of a chart proving most useful in helping the trader get a feel for where major turning points might occur. Given this success in using charts to spot turnaround points, some might wonder why an analysis of the degree of a market's balance (i.e., range extensions, extremes, TPO count) is even necessary. Why couldn't a trader simply have bought Lumber when it intersected the trend line on the 17th of May? To answer simply, while charting analysis is quite helpful in determining possible pivotal price areas in the markets, the turns or price changes which the charts lead one to expect at these points do not always occur. Many times, the trend line that can be expected to halt a price decline or restrain a bear market rally

**EXHIBIT C**

| | JUNE 1 | JUNE 2 | JUNE 3 | JUNE 6 | JUNE 7 | JUNE 8 |
|---|---|---|---|---|---|---|
| 58.00 | | | | | | |
| 57.95 | | | | | | |
| 57.90 | | | | | | |
| 57.85 | | | | | | |
| 57.80 | | F | | | | |
| 57.75 | | F | | | | |
| 57.70 | K | F | | | | |
| 57.65 | J | F | | | | |
| 57.60 | JKQ | F | | | | |
| 57.55 | JK | CFG | | | JULY | |
| 57.50 | JK | CFG | | | PORK BELLIES | |
| 57.45 | JK | CFG | | | | |
| 57.40 | J | CFG | | | | |
| 57.35 | J | CEFG | | | | |
| 57.30 | J | CEFG | | | | |
| 57.25 | J | CEFG | | | | |
| 57.20 | J | CDEFGHIJ | | F | | |
| 57.15 | DJ | CDEGHJK | | F | | |
| 57.10 | CDJ | CDGHJK | | F | | |
| 57.05 | CDJ | CDGHJKQ | | F | | |
| 57.00 | CDJ | CDHJK | | F | | |
| 56.95 | CDJ | CDHJ | | F | | |
| 56.90 | CDIJ | CDHIJ | | F | | |
| 56.85 | CDIJ | DHIJ | | F | | |
| 56.80 | CDGHIJ | DHIJ | | F | | |
| 56.75 | CDFGHIJ | HIJ | | FGIJ | | |
| 56.70 | CDEFGHIJ | HIJ | | FIJ | | |
| 56.65 | CDEFGHIJ | IJ | | FGIJ | | |
| 56.60 | CDEFGHIJ | IJ | | FGIJ | | |
| 56.55 | CDEFGH | I | | FGIJ | | |
| 56.50 | DEFGH | | C | FGIJ | | |
| 56.45 | DEH | | C | FGIJ | | |
| 56.40 | DH | | CD | FGHIJ | | |
| 56.35 | H | | CDE | EFGHIJ | | |
| 56.30 | H | | CDE | EFGHIJ | | |
| 56.25 | H | | CDE | EGHJK | C | |
| 56.20 | | | CDE | EGHJK | C | |
| 56.15 | | | CDE | EGHJK | C | |
| 56.10 | | | CEJ | CDEGHJK | C | |
| 56.05 | | | CEJ | CDEGHK | C | |
| 56.00 | | | CEEJ | CDEH | C | |
| 55.95 | | | EJ | CDH | C | |
| 55.90 | | | EJ | CDH | C | |
| 55.85 | | | EHJ | CDJ | | |
| 55.80 | | | EFHJ | CDJ | CDJ | |
| 55.75 | | | EFHIJ | CDJ | CDJ | |
| 55.70 | | | EFHIJ | CJ | CDJ | |
| 55.65 | | | EFHIJ | | D | |
| 55.60 | | | EFGHIJK | | D | |
| 55.55 | | | FGHIJKQ | | DE | |
| 55.50 | | | FGHIJK | | DEI | |
| 55.45 | | | FGHIJK | | DEFI | |
| 55.40 | | | FGIJ | | DEFGIJ | |
| 55.35 | | | FGIJ | | DEFGIJ | |
| 55.30 | | | | | | |
| 55.25 | | | | | | |
| 55.20 | | | | | | C |
| 55.15 | | | | | | CDIJ |
| 55.10 | | | | | | CDIJ |
| 55.05 | | | | | | CDIJ |
| 55.00 | | | | | | CDIJ |
| 54.95 | | | | | | CDIJ |
| 54.90 | | | | | | CDIJ |
| 54.85 | | | | | | CDE |
| 54.80 | | | | | | CDE |
| 54.75 | | | | | | CDE |
| 54.70 | | | | | | CDE |
| 54.65 | | | | | | CEJ |
| 54.60 | | | | | | CEJ |
| 54.55 | | | | | | E |
| 54.50 | | | | | | E |
| 54.45 | | | | | | E |
| 54.40 | | | | | | E |
| 54.35 | | | | | | E |
| 54.30 | | | | | | E |
| 54.25 | | | | | | E |
| 54.20 | | | | | | E |
| 54.15 | | | | | | E |
| 54.10 | | | | | | E |
| 54.05 | | | | | | E |
| 54.00 | | | | | | E |
| 53.95 | | | | | | E |
| 53.90 | | | | | | E |

fails to do so. Furthermore, trendlines or figure
patterns are often inexact in their appearance.
The exact point at which a price turn may be
expected can be difficult to determine. As a result,
market action slightly beyond the exact spots
identified on the chart may place one in a bad
trade or encourage exiting the market just before
the turnaround takes place. The key, then, is to
identify whether the market is in a balanced
posture and could hold technical support.

For an example of how charting analysis alone
can be deceptive, refer to Exhibit C, a chart of July
Pork Bellies for the month of June. Coming off a
cyclical low in May, Bellies had rallied to 55.50 by
May 15, pulled back to 53.00 by May 23, rallied to
57.50 by early June, and, following this top, were
selling off. Applying charting analysis to the Belly
market, a trader would deduce that the trend line
(connecting the lows on May 4, May 10, and May
26) would stop the decline and that the market
would hold at the 53.75 level. Had the trader
relied solely on these charting data and placed an
order to enter the market when the target price
was reached on June 8, the results would have
been disastrous. Disregarding technical support,
the Bellies blew through the 53.75 mark,
proceeding to go limit down. Within two weeks,
this market had sold off more than 12 basis
points.

Could melding market-generated information
with technical analysis have helped the trader
avoid disaster with this trade? Look at the profiles
found in Exhibit D. On June 1, Bellies posted their
intraday high at 57.70 during a neutral day (range
extensions on both top and bottom), and closed on
their highs. As previously discussed, neutral days
can be "test" days, signals that change is highly
probable. On June 2, the market again tested the

tops on another neutral day. The profile of the 2nd exhibits a strong selling extreme left during F period. By the end of the day, the market had traded down and closed with basically unchanged value from the 1st. On June 3, the market opened lower and entered into a trend day down. Given the back-to-back test days, this action was no surprise. However, on the 6th the Bellies popped up to once again look at the highs (they reached 57.25) but a wave of responsive selling drove them down, leaving a large F period selling extreme. On June 7, the market again experienced a trend day down, taking prices to 55.35 by close. At this point, many a chartist who was looking to buy at the trend line intersection was eagerly awaiting the chance to get long. However, prices had not yet reached the intersection point and the Market Logician, also aware of the trend line intersection point, was waiting to see definite signs that the market was slowing its selling pace.

On June 8, the market opened on its highs and immediately entered into a trend day down. The profile for this day, shows a market that did pause briefly during the D and E periods at the 54.60 to 54.85 level (the trend line intersection point). However, the market remained in a one timeframe mode and blew through this area of support. Once through this level, the market was in a freefall (notice the single prints during the E period). The only thing that stopped the selling on the 8th was the daily price limit at 52.875. Clearly, prior to the chartist's point of expected support, the market gave definite and distinct signals that it was not balanced and that it could not be expected to stop at the trend line intersection point. When the market reached the target price range, responsive buying did not dominate the market. Any trader watching this markedly imbalanced activity would immediately know that the market was in a selling mode and that entering into any long positions would be foolhardy. In fact, the action on the 8th (and follow-through on the 9th) made it clear that the initiating sellers were in control and that the door might be open to shorting the market.

While it would be nice if charting analysis consistently yielded infallible results, it is a simple truth that charting, at best, provides only a rough guide to price areas that may be pivotal to trend direction and continuation. When used as a support tool for the logical analysis of market-generated information, charts do provide utility and value. However, when taken alone, or in conjunction with other price-generated technical data, they offer only suspect information and sketchy trading results.

### Support and Resistance

One of the most basic tenets of technical work is that price tends to move directionally until it encounters an area where, for one reason or another, market participants feel that current price is fairly valued and the trend action should stop. The price areas where trending price action is halted are known as support and resistance areas. These areas are crucial to most technical traders; they give a good indication of where prices will slow down and possibly reverse direction. This book has referred to the ability of the other timeframe buyers and sellers to contain the market through an increased level of competition at attractive price levels. Thus, it is the group of other timeframe buyers which provides support to the market and other timeframe sellers who act to give resistance.

One way to conceptualize support and resistance is by referring to a bar chart, Exhibit E, a daily bar chart of August Gold. A technician, examining this chart in early April would have observed that Gold had recently made a bottom in late February, rallied to the 468.00 level in March, and, as of the first week of April had begun a break. Seeing this activity, the technician (assuming he was bullish the Gold) would have been drawn to look for a spot where Gold had found support by ceasing to break in the past. An area such as this would provide support for the market, possibly halting the current decline in Gold prices and reversing the trend.

During the first two weeks of February, Gold had found good support at the 450.00 to 455.00 area. Again, in early March, the market found this price area served as resistance (old support areas often become new resistance areas) when the market tried to rally off its lows. Noting this area of support/resistance, the technical trader would have deduced that Gold could find support at the 455.00 area and possibly reverse direction. It then came as no great surprise that the market, trading down to the 454.00 area the week of April 4 found support in this area and reversed direction. Had the trader used this form of technical analysis to exit a short position or establish a new long position, the method would have proven quite effective.

Not to be overwhelmed by the success in the first example, the trader must be cautious. There are many times when traditional support/ resistance analysis fails to provide reliable trading conclusions. Looking again at the Gold, note the two week period June 13 through June 20. The Gold market had again traded down to the 454.00 support area, bounced briefly, rallied slightly, and then resumed its downward course. The technician, expecting the 450.00 support area to hold, might be moved to exit short positions and

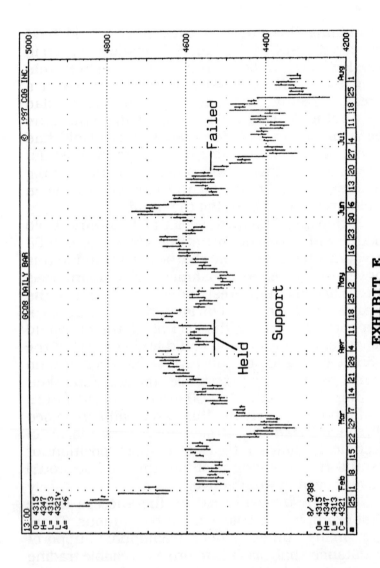

**EXHIBIT E**

enter long positions. Without the benefit of knowing precisely how the market is trading internally (are the dominant other timeframe traders buyers or seller?, is there responsive buying?), the technician would be sentenced to simply position and pray. To the dismay of the technician, the market moved through the support area and traded to much lower levels. Had a short position been exited or a new long established based on the support/resistance analysis, the technician would have suffered a several hundred dollar per contract loss.

How can the analysis of support and resistance be combined with the use of profiles and market-generated information to provide enhanced results? Refer again to the Gold chart. Using the support area at 454.00 merely as a reference point — an area where price trend change is likely to occur — the trader could then direct his attention to the profile to observe whether the responsive trader becomes active and reverses the market.

As has been noted in the past, it is the presence of the responsive trader which first brings about a change in market direction. His presence is the tipoff that the market is susceptible to a reversal. This is an opportune time to outline precisely what types of profile activity constitute responsive behavior.

Illustrated in Exhibit F are three basic types of profile activity which are characteristic of the responsive trader entering the market. The examples refer to responsive buying activity, although the inverse would also be true for selling activity:

## 1. Buying Extreme

This form of responsive behavior should be familiar, as it is plotted as an element of the Long

Term Market Activity Chart. When sellers drive prices down far enough during one TPO period that the price level is overwhelmingly rejected as being too low, responsive buyers step into the market and quickly move prices back up into the normal range of the day. This type of behavior often occurs quite rapidly and is often significant to the

longer-term trend.

### 2. Failed Auction

When a market extends the range beyond the initial balance, in effect the market participants have begun a new auction, concluding that the initial price level was no longer appropriate given the current imbalance and that prices must be moved to facilitate trade. Should an auction be started and not gather sufficient velocity, a situation known as a "failed auction" is created. A failed auction can be easily recognized as a meager range extension with no follow-through. It is caused by activity moving into an area where responsive traders step in and push prices back into the initial balance area, containing the market. Oftentimes a failed auction can trigger a sharp move in the direction opposite the failed auction.

### 3. Double Print Extremes

By definition, an extreme must only consist of a series of single print TPO's. However, many times a market will probe to an area where price is rejected but the time period changes from one letter to another before price moves back into the intial balance area. When this occurs, the market forms a double print extreme. Though not typically plotted on the LTMA Chart, the double print extreme is a form of responsive activity and should be credited as such.

## Exhibit B

| | | |
|---|---|---|
| | BCDEF | ABCDE |
| AG | ABCDE | ABCD |
| ABFG | ABCD | ABC |
| ABEF | ABC | ABC |
| ABDE | CDE | BC |
| CDE | CDE | BC |
| CD | CD | BC |
| C | | |
| C | | |
| C | | |
| **Buying Extreme** | **Failed Auction** | **Double Print Extreme** |

EXHIBIT F

Copyright 1984 CBOT

By noting the above mentioned forms of
responsive profile activity, the technical trader
can greatly enhance his success in using support
and resistance area as a basic guide to trading
suspected reversal areas.

*Relative Strength*

Another variation of technical analysis, relative
strength, is best known and most frequently used
to indicate when intermediate to long term
changes in trend can be expected. The relative
strength index measures the underlying market
strength at a specific price area, and then
compares that reading with other readings
obtained when the market traded in the price
area. The relative strength index is calculated
based on the average "net change" of closing
prices for the preceding 14 number of time units
prior to the time of calculation. For example, the
longer term RSI measures the average for the past
14 days. Each day, the amount the market closes
up or down is taken with the same closing figure
for the 13 days previous. "Up" closes and "down"
closes are grouped independently, averaged, and
run through a series of calculations to arrive at a
number between 1 and 100 which defines how
strong the underlying momentum of the market is
at that time.

Relative strength index analysts believe that
markets, when involved in strong trending moves,
begin to reach a first stage exhaustion point when
their RSI reaches either a level of 30 (downtrend)
or 70 (uptrend). Once these levels are reached, the
analyst then watches prices for a setback or rally
in the market. Once the rally or setback occurs it
is typically followed by another move, or possibly
to prices even beyond those reached originally at
the exhaustion point. When the second rally or
break ends, the RSI watcher then compares the

index reading at the open of the second rally or break with that achieved in the first move. Many times the RSI on the second move is substantially lower or higher than it was on the first move. This occurs in spite of the fact that prices in the second move matched or surpassed those in the first. This phenomenon, known as "divergence," tells the RSI analyst that a trend change can be expected. This is because even though a market made higher highs or lower lows on the second rally effort, the internal strength or weakness of the market, "relative" to the first rally or break, is substantially lower (on a rally) or higher (on a break).

To help explain how RSI is used in a practical sense, the following will present an example of how a technician's trading decision-making might be structured using this measurement.

Exhibit G is the daily bar chart for December Cotton. From February through April, Cotton had been breaking and, on April 21, the market finally made a bottom at 54.90. (This is a closing price. Since all RSI numbers are based on closing prices they will be used in the example.) Beginning on April 22, Cotton began a four week rally until it made a primary move high on May 17 at 62.60. On that date, the RSI was 84.5. This figure was well above the 70 level (exhaustion level for rallies) and RSI analysts were undoubtedly looking for a setback. During the next ten days, the market did setback to a low of 59.08. The RSI at this point also retreated to 45.7.

Undaunted, Cotton then launched a secondary rally which carried it to a peak of 67.90 on the 20th of June. Examining the corresponding RSI for that same date, the index analyst found that the figure was only 72.5. Although the market on the second leg of its rally carried more than 500

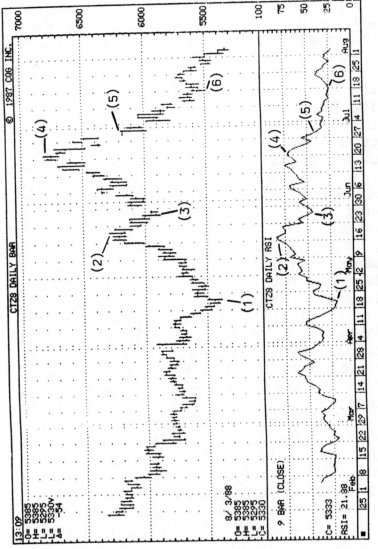

**EXHIBIT G**

points higher than the highest point reached in the primary leg of the rally, the RSI, even with the market 500 points higher, was some 12 points lower than the corresponding apex of the primary move. This "divergence" between the higher price and not higher relative strength measurement told the technician that the market was internally weak at higher prices and that a trend reversal might be forthcoming.

Ready to sell short the market, the RSI analyst focused his attention on daily index readings in relation to the level reached on May 26 (see point (3) on the chart). The RSI on this date was the "critical point" for the trade. If and when the market traded down to prices which resulted in an RSI lower that that seen on the lowest point of the break which occurred between the primary and secondary leg of the rally, then the turnaround in the trend was confirmed and it was time to get short.

On June 29, Cotton reached a relative strength level of 39.3 and confirmed the trend reversal. The following day, on the 30th, the RSI analyst sold the opening, establishing a position at 61.70. During the next three weeks the market continued to break until it reached a low of 54.95 on July 18th. The RSI technician was able to take some 675 points out of a very defined (from an RSI standpoint) trade.

Despite the apparent merits of RSI analysis, the employment of the index as a primary trading decision tool does have its drawbacks. Perhaps the most glaring failure of the RSI is its inability to recommend good trade location. Good trade location, it should be stressed, is absolutely critical to the success of any trade.

By examining Exhibit H, the daily bar chart of the September 1988 S & P, one can clearly see how the RSI can fail to provide good trade location, and when markets are choppy, how this poor trade location can result in losses.

On May 23, the S & P made a low at 252.45. The market then set out on a three week rally, ultimately reaching a closing high on June 15 at 276.95. The RSI at this point was 74.04. In the subsequent week, the S & P broke to the 270.00 level and again rallied, matching and surpassing the primary leg high. The new high on June 22 at 277.95, though some 100 points higher than on the 15th, achieved a relative strength index of only 68.2 (some 6 points lower). This divergence signaled a possible reversal in trend.

The reversal was apparently confirmed on June 27 when the RSI crossed the "critical" point established on June 22. On the following day, the RSI trader then established a short position on the opening at 270.60. However, instead of continuing to sell off, the market rallied sharply, putting the short position down some 900 points in less than 5 days. Though useful in a trending market, RSI use proved ineffective while the market remained in a trading range.

How would the analysis of market-generated information provide insight to the RSI trader? Once the divergence between price and RSI was spotted in the September S & P on June 22 and the technical analyst was alerted to a possible reversal, the analyst of the Long Term Market Activity Chart and daily profiles would have wondered whether the market would continue to break when it reached the "critical" point, or whether the responsive traders would step in and rally the market, leaving it in a trading range? Unless a trader can see the emergence of the other timeframe trader when a position is considered,

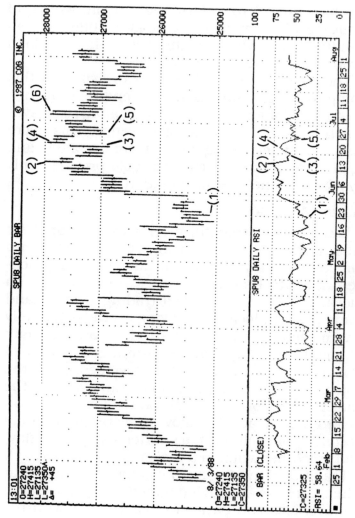

**EXHIBIT H**

he has no micro information upon which to
evaluate whether the move he is "going with" will
continue, or whether the move has a high
probability of ending abruptly.

The conclusion which can be drawn from this
comparison is that relative strength, though a
useful tool for longer-term market analysis, leaves
much to be desired in a micro sense. This micro
analysis, determining market continuation and
good trade location, requires tools provided only
by market-generated information.

*Moving Averages*

Like relative strength, moving average analysis
aids traders in identifying changes in trend
direction and momentum. Many of the self-
described technical "systems" rely heavily on
moving averages for overall trading strategy and
trade position location. Moving averages typically
are measured in 4 day, 9 day, and 18 day
segments and are simply running averages of
closing prices for the duration specified. Since the
objective of the averages is to capture visually the
changes in short term trend direction in relation
to longer term activity, moving averages naturally
become more volatile in a shorter span (i.e., 4 day)
and smoother when in a longer span (i.e., 18 day).

Traditional moving average analysis posits that
when a market is moving directionally in a trend,
the averages run parallel to each other with the
shorter term leading the way and longer term
lagging behind. When a market initiates price
activity which may spell a change in direction, the
shorter term averages respond first and
ultimately, when the trend has presumably
changed, cross over the long term averages,
confirming a signal.

A graphic example of how moving average
technicians employ these tools is found in Exhibit

I, the daily bar chart of September 1988 Treasury Bonds. In early March, Bonds topped out in the 93-00 area and began to break. On March 10, the 9 day Moving Average (solid line) crossed over the 18 day average (dotted line). To the moving average trader, this event signaled the reversal of the trend and dictated it was time to establish a short position. The market was sold at the open of March 11 at 90-22. Immediately, the position was a loser as the market rallied for the next 5 days. However, if the trader held the position he would ultimately profit, since the market then turned and continued the break.

The only other time the market moved against the trade was in early April, as the first leg of the break ended and the market underwent a correction rally. However, the rally was never of sufficient strength to push the 9 day average back over the 18. This event would have signaled to the trader that he consider covering the position.

In early June, the break finally ended. On the 7th, the 9 day finally crossed the 18 day, signaling the end of the trend. The moving average trader then covered the position at 87-10, realizing a profit of more than 3 basis points.

Like the relative strength index, moving averages have great utility for one attempting to identify the onset of major trends. Unfortunately, moving averages fall short of the mark when markets either do not follow through in major trends and perform what might be termed "swing trades," or else become choppy, without clear trend direction.

Take for example the activity documented earlier in August Gold (see Exhibit J). After a sharp rally, Gold moved into a trading range in early April. When the MA analyst observed the break which began the last week of March and

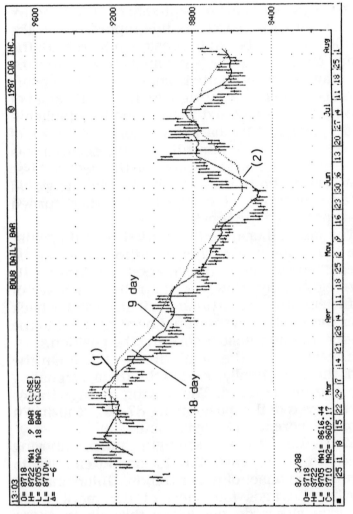

**EXHIBIT I**

which ultimately moved the 9 day average below the 18 day on April 13, he was moved to short the market at 456 area on the open of the 14th. However, since the market was in a trading range and not a trend, the trade went against the MA analyst and eventually took him out of the market when the 9 day crossed the 18 day to the upside some 7 days later. In fact, the MA trader, over the course of the next three months, would have been directed to position some five times, each resulting in whipsaw action and a lack of trend follow-through. Undoubtedly, MA analysis failed to provide results when markets were choppy.

Perhaps the greatest flaw in trading systems based on moving average is their inability to provide good trade location. Like relative strength, use of the averages has a built-in time lag, a delay in price trend recognition. Even when accurate in diagnosing a change in market direction, moving averages dictate trade establishment well after the market has turned and a great deal of the initial price swing has passed.

Moving averages, as well as other traditional tools of technical analysis, can be very effective when employed as a supplement to the use of market-generated information. With them, a trader can develop comprehensive decision-making methodology for ascertaining trend identification as well as garnering good trade location. In essence, macro technical indicators serve as an "index" to the markets. Used in conjunction with other tools including the Long Term Market Activity Chart, these indicators give the trader a general idea of possible locations where turning points in the market may occur. Many technical tools actually serve best to merely confirm that a turn in the market had already occurred. After general reference points have been

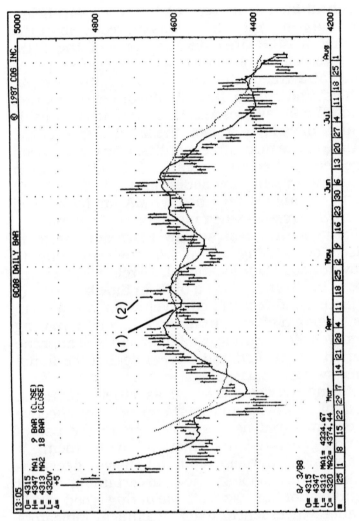

**EXHIBIT J**

determined, the identification of the "micro" elements — precisely if and when the market will turn — can be ascertained through examination of daily profiles.

# Chapter 16

# Market Analysis:
# Deutsche Mark

As mentioned earlier, participation in the financial markets can be likened to managing a business. The challenge facing the businessman is the identical challenge of the trader/investor: to manage and to make decisions based on an analysis of an ever-changing flow of two forms of information. The first flow is fundamental information, supply and demand data outside the marketplace, and the second is market-generated information. To logically analyze the data that result from a market-generated information flow in the financial markets requires many of the insights presented in this book.

An analysis of one market on a day-by-day basis illustrates this challenge most graphically. The market, continually ebbing and flowing in an on-going interplay between buyers and sellers, challenges the trader to:

· track where (at what price) and how (responsively or in an initiating manner) the other timeframe buyer and seller groups react to an opportunity

· analyze the degree of balance or imbalance present, thereby determining who is currently more dominant between the other timeframe buyers and sellers

· decide whether to buy or sell
· find the ideal trade location
· place short term information into a framework
that allows a longer term conclusion to be drawn.
This list is most important for the longer term
trader.

This enables the trader to decide whether to
enter a position, add to it or hold it, lighten the
exposure or look to exit the market altogether.

This day-by-day analysis of the Deutsche Mark
depicts the weighting of market-generated
information. Issues important to the day trader
are listed under the "micro" heading. An analysis
which weights each day's activity within the
context of the previous day's activity, drawing
conclusions applicable for longer term conviction
is listed under "macro" analysis. This narrative
will describe the thoughts that should cross the
mind of both the short term and longer term
trader as they interpret the market's behavior and
structure a decision-making process around that
interpretation. The weekly chart shows a long-
term uptrend beginning in March of 1985. As of
the end of this chart, the 30-month-old bull
market is mature, yet there is nothing that
indicates an attractive selling opportunity for the
long-term trader. Rather, the trend is the bull's
friend. The question begged by a cursory look at
this weekly chart is simply whether or not this
market — clearly in an uptrend — can still be
bought. For those who already are long, has the
market moved far enough for them to begin taking
profits? Again, the mature bull market creates a
quandary: while price is above value over the
larger sample size, the quick and pronounced
directional move which usually occurs at the tail
end of a mature market also provides the greatest
opportunity for substantial returns. Thus,

correctly identifying signs that the market is continuing the trend versus signs that it has already climaxed is very rewarding.

The next chart, the LTMAC of October 1-16, 1987, displays a strong market in an imbalanced condition brought on by aggressive other timeframe buying. Note the preponderance of initiating buying activity on the right-hand side of the chart and the marked absence of corresponding initiating selling activity. In addition to displaying the prototypical bull market feature of prices moving higher over time, the Deutsche Mark at this time tends to close strongly on the week. The 2nd, the 9th, and the 16th each settle their respective week's activity toward at least the top third of the week's high-low range. Note the two largest value area ranges occur from higher, initiating activity.

Before we begin the day-by-day analysis, it should be noted that an analysis of the Deutsche Mark was chosen in large part because the currency market is a 24-hour market, different from the vast majority of markets which feature a single time zone primary market. In the interbank/currency markets, trading in three distinct time zones — the Far Eastern, the London and the New York/IMM — makes up the entire day's activity. Unlike many of the other markets which are traded around the clock, the New York time zone during which IMM futures markets trade does not comprise the majority of the worldwide currency market's transactional activity. Thus, as the following exercise examines only the New York/IMM time zone, please note that day structures apparent in markets which transact the bulk of world trade (for example, the New York Stock Exchange for IBM, the International Monetary Market for Eurodollar futures, etc.) are not necessarily going to be seen in the same percentages. In other words, the following will examine but a slice of the total market-generated information, but aside from a skewing of day structure behavior, the analysis will be identical to that which would apply to a non-24-hour market. For ease of analysis, we will consider the initial balance to be the first hour's trade (Y-Z period) even though we would often look to ranges established in the Far Eastern time zone to establish the initial balance in many cases. Also note that non-facilitation (non-trend), trend-type and bell-shaped neutral day (without as great a significance attached to them) are the day structures seen in the New York/IMM currency futures. Another behavior particular to the currencies is that trend days tend as often as not to close in the middle of developing value, in sharp contrast to the prototypical trend day seen in non-24-hour markets, which almost always settles on the extreme. An explanation of this may lie in the fact that the close of the IMM currency futures is not a market-imposed timeframe. The bank's "book is passed" to dealers in the next time zone.

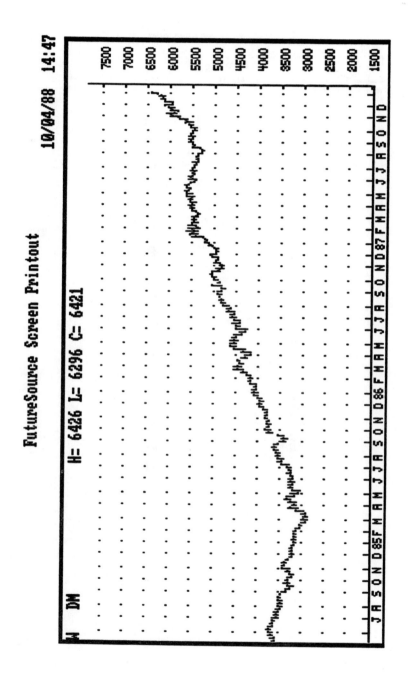

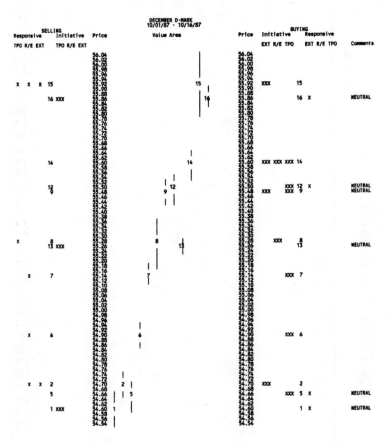

**10-19 Micro Analysis**: Following a quiet initial balance, the market extends the range up in A period and a single print is formed in B. Often, a single print range extension (in either direction) can signal a failure to continue, an indication that the market may probe in the opposite direction. In this case the market does extend down — in E period, but fails again to continue beyond that. The market builds value around the range of the initial balance. Note the degree of balance and the profile's resemblance to a bell curve.

**10-19 Macro Analysis**: As havoc played on in the other financial markets due to the stock market crash, the currency markets were fairly quiet. They have been in a dramatic bull market and have had a significant run caused by an active other timeframe buying imbalance. But the market is an ebb and flow between buyers and sellers. Having rallied, the strength early in the week, plus the balanced look of this day's profile leaves the market susceptible to falling back for a while if other timeframe sellers enter and dominate activity.

**Note — Prices are on the leftmost vertical axis, to the right of which are two rows of numbers. The row next to price denotes the number of half hour segments during which that particular price traded. The third column represents the number of trades (not by contract) that took place at each price. The last column is a visual representation of price formulated over time organized with a bell curve, normal distribution. The black lines represent where 70% of the volume on that day's activity occurred as measured both by the number of Time-Price Opportunities (TPOs) and by the number (as opposed to volume) of trades taking place at each price. This 70% calculation, the first standard deviation of the normal distribution, is the market's perception of value on any particular day.**

TRADING SIMULATOR - Based on the CBOT Market Profile*

DM 1287 13:20:08 56.74  O 56.69  H 56.92  L 56.59  V 1027 TB 73ˉ70  TV 441ˉ527
       10/19/87

```
56.92   0    0
56.91   1    5   B
56.90   2    7   AB
56.89   2   11   AB
56.88   2   17   AB
56.87   3   20   ABD
56.86   4   22   ABCD
56.85   4   22   ABCD
56.84   4   32   ABCD
56.83   4   42   ABCD
56.82   4   40   ABCD
56.81   4   30   ABCD
56.80   6   18   ABCDJK
56.79   5   24   ACDJK
56.78   4   28   ADJK
56.77   6   33   yzADJK
56.76   6   40   yzADJK
56.75   6   48  - yzADJK
56.74   7   59   yzADGJX
56.73   8   56   yzADEGHJ
56.72   8   51   yzADEGHJ
56.71   8   53   yzDEGHIJ
56.70   8   49   yzDEGHIJ
56.69   6   38   OEGHIJ
56.68   6   24   yEGHIJ
56.67   5   23   EFGHI
56.66   5   34   EFGHI
56.65   5   39   EFGHI
56.64   4   37   EFHI
56.63   4   43   EFHI
56.62   4   42   EFHI
56.61   4   26   EFHI
56.60   3   11   EFI
56.59   1    1   E
```

**10-20 Micro Analysis**: Opening with a distinctly wide Y-Z initial balance, the market finds a
selling imbalance early that causes the market to
fall away quickly and violently in A period, nearly
doubling the initial balance and nearing the 5500
level. The bounce that forms the buying extreme
indicates that other timeframe buyers are interested at lower prices.

**10-20 Macro Analysis**: Are weak and nervous
longs being shaken out of the market by the violent A period break, or is this significant new selling, selling which can be expected to continue at
increasingly lower prices for at least several sessions to come and possibly more? If it is this second activity, the market should not have bounced,
but should have continued lower, since the other
timeframe participants as a rule enter a market
slowly and steadily over a period of days and
weeks. The fact that value and volume develop on
the top half of the day's range indicates strength,
as does the degree of bounce that this market
experiences. Note that the market rallies back
from the lows long before the stock market
regrouped on this day.

TRADING SIMULATOR - Based on the CBOT Market Profile*

DM 1287 13:20:26 55.51  O 56.00  H 56.00  L 55.05  V 1326 TB 130ˆ100TV 869ˆ392
         10/20/87

```
56.00    0     0
55.98    0     0
55.96    1     1     y
55.94    1     1     y
55.92    2     2     G
55.90    3    12     yG
55.88    4    18     yG
55.86    6    25     yzG
55.84    6    32     yzG
55.82    8    55     yzGH
55.80    8    80     yzGH
55.78    8    37     yzGH
55.76    8    52     yzGH
55.74    8    46     yzGH
55.72   10    34     yzGHI
55.70    8    35     yzDGI
55.68    6    35     zGHI
55.66    8    42     zDGHI
55.64   15    47     zCDFGHIJ
55.62   16    83     zCDEFGHIJ
55.60   18    88     zBCDEFGHIJ
55.58   14    88     zBCDEFJ
55.56   15   120     zABCDEFJ
55.54   15    76     zABCDEFJK
55.52   13    48  -  zABCDJK
55.50   13    57     zABCDGX
55.48    5    18     ABC
55.46    4    12     AB
55.44    4     9     AB
55.42    3     3     AB
55.40    4    12     AB
55.38    4    26     AB
55.36    4    27     AB
55.34    3    15     AB
55.32    2    11     A
55.30    2    15     A
55.28    2    11     A
55.26    1     5     A
55.24    1    12     A
55.22    1     2     A
55.20    2    11     A
55.18    2     3     A
55.16    2     4     A
55.14    1     6     A
55.12    1     1     A
55.10    2     5     A
55.08    1     1     A
55.06    1     1     A
```

**10-21 Micro Analysis**: After a higher opening, the market scores a quieter initial balance than the 20th. This can be expected after so active a previous session; the other timeframe participants need to "rest." In emerging markets the rest may take several days whereas in active and volatile markets, where activity is sped up, rest can be as short as the first few hours of the session following the major imbalance. The selling range extension in A, confirmed not by a single TPO but by continuation in C, indicates weakness for the day. The level of volatile yet directional activity is to be expected given the one timeframe nature of this maturing market. The consistently lower lows, the weak close and the lone TPOs in C period display a trend day structure. This day is imbalanced and in the hands of the other timeframe seller.

**10-21 Macro Analysis**: Even though this is a strong selling day, the market fails to probe below the previous session lows, a sign that selling is not increasing at the lower levels, something to be expected if the previous session's selling was caused by new selling. It is still early in the week and the trend is up, so we would be surprised to see the buying that is supporting the market at these lower levels supporting the market at higher levels over coming sessions, especially by the week's settlement.

TRADING SIMULATOR - Based on the CBOT Market Profile*

DM 1287 13:19:36 55.26  O 55.70  H 55.79  L 55.23  V  921 TB 113ˇ52 TV 177ˇ704
        10/21/87

| Price | | | |
|---|---|---|---|
| 55.79 | 0 | 0 | |
| 55.78 | 1 | 3 | y |
| 55.77 | 1 | 9 | y |
| 55.76 | 2 | 11 | yz |
| 55.75 | 2 | 12 | yz |
| 55.74 | 2 | 20 | yz |
| 55.73 | 3 | 18 | yzB |
| 55.72 | 3 | 15 | yzB |
| 55.71 | 4 | 26 | yzAB |
| 55.70 | 5 | 32 | OzABC |
| 55.69 | 5 | 30 | yzABC |
| 55.68 | 5 | 40 | yzABC |
| 55.67 | 4 | 37 | zABC |
| 55.66 | 3 | 17 | zAC |
| 55.65 | 2 | 7 | AC |
| 55.64 | 2 | 4 | AC |
| 55.63 | 1 | 3 | C |
| 55.62 | 1 | 3 | C |
| 55.61 | 3 | 5 | CDE |
| 55.60 | 3 | 10 | CDE |
| 55.59 | 3 | 10 | CDE |
| 55.58 | 3 | 13 | CDE |
| 55.57 | 4 | 13 | CDEF |
| 55.56 | 4 | 16 | CDEF |
| 55.55 | 4 | 23 | CDEF |
| 55.54 | 3 | 23 | DEF |
| 55.53 | 3 | 17 | DEF |
| 55.52 | 3 | 15 | DEF |
| 55.51 | 3 | 10 | DEF |
| 55.50 | 3 | 9 | DEF |
| 55.49 | 3 | 7 | DEF |
| 55.48 | 2 | 5 | DF |
| 55.47 | 3 | 13 | DFG |
| 55.46 | 3 | 20 | DFG |
| 55.45 | 3 | 17 | DFG |
| 55.44 | 3 | 19 | DFG |
| 55.43 | 3 | 21 | DFG |
| 55.42 | 3 | 16 | DFG |
| 55.41 | 3 | 18 | DFG |
| 55.40 | 4 | 17 | DFGH |
| 55.39 | 5 | 11 | DFGHJ |
| 55.38 | 5 | 14 | DFGHJ |
| 55.37 | 4 | 13 | FGHJ |
| 55.36 | 4 | 13 | FGHJ |
| 55.35 | 5 | 20 | FGHIJ |
| 55.34 | 4 | 23 | GHIJ |
| 55.33 | 4 | 28 | GHIJ |
| 55.32 | 4 | 28 | GHIJ |
| 55.31 | 3 | 30 | HIJ |
| 55.30 | 3 | 28 | HIJ |
| 55.29 | 3 | 21 | HIJ |
| 55.28 | 3 | 18 | HIJ |
| 55.27 | 2 | 21 | IJ |
| 55.26 | 3 | 26 | IJX |
| 55.25 | 3 | 16 | IJK |
| 55.24 | 2 | 5 | IK |
| 55.23 | 1 | 1 | I |

*CBOT Market Profile and Market Profile are registered trademarks of the
Chicago Board of Trade
Copyright Board of Trade of the City of Chicago 1984.  All Rights Reserved.

**10-22 Micro Analysis**: Opening at the low end of the previous session's value, the market has an active initial balance and finds good other time-frame buying which causes a buying extreme and then a strong buying range extension. While good buying is present, good selling also is present, illustrated by the fact that the market does not hold the levels reached in the A period rally, and later comes back to trade in and close at the level of what was earlier the buying extreme.

**10-22 Macro Analysis**: The past two days illus-trate a nervous and very active market, symp-tomatic of a market in a maturing trend. With both other timeframe buying and selling present on this day, the question remains: which is the dominant force? Given that the market is volatile, and given that both the LTMAC and the weekly charts indicate the market has been in a trend, plus the fact that the buying imbalance defined this day by the active range extension, we expect to see other timeframe buying dominating, but the market needs to demonstrate this.

TRADING SIMULATOR - Based on the CBOT Market Profile*

DM 1287 13:19:55 55.33  O 55.36  H 55.80  L 55.31  V  893 TB 84^59  TV 616^231
         10/22/87

| | | | |
|---|---|---|---|
| 55.80 | 0 | 0 | |
| 55.79 | 0 | 0 | |
| 55.78 | -1 | 1 | A |
| 55.77 | 0 | 0 | |
| 55.76 | 1 | 1 | A |
| 55.75 | 2 | 4 | AB |
| 55.74 | 2 | 4 | AB |
| 55.73 | 2 | 3 | AB |
| 55.72 | 1 | 4 | B |
| 55.71 | 2 | 5 | AB |
| 55.70 | 2 | 15 | AB |
| 55.69 | 2 | 12 | AB |
| 55.68 | 2 | 15 | AB |
| 55.67 | 2 | 15 | AB |
| 55.66 | 2 | 17 | AB |
| 55.65 | 2 | 13 | AB |
| 55.64 | 2 | 12 | AB |
| 55.63 | 2 | 14 | AB |
| 55.62 | 3 | 23 | ABC |
| 55.61 | 3 | 28 | ABC |
| 55.60 | 3 | 28 | ABC |
| 55.59 | 3 | 25 | ABC |
| 55.58 | 2 | 23 | AC |
| 55.57 | 2 | 23 | AC |
| 55.56 | 2 | 20 | AC |
| 55.55 | 2 | 9 - | AC |
| 55.54 | 2 | 5 | AC |
| 55.53 | 2 | 8 | AC |
| 55.52 | 2 | 9 | AC |
| 55.51 | 3 | 7 | zAC |
| 55.50 | 5 | 14 | zACDE |
| 55.49 | 5 | 20 | zACDE |
| 55.48 | 5 | 22 | zCDEH |
| 55.47 | 5 | 20 | zCDEH |
| 55.46 | 5 | 23 | zCDEH |
| 55.45 | 5 | 34 | zCDEH |
| 55.44 | 7 | 43 | zDEFGHI |
| 55.43 | 6 | 34 | zDEGHI |
| 55.42 | 7 | 28 | zDEFGHI |
| 55.41 | 6 | 34 | zDFGHI |
| 55.40 | 5 | 46 | zFGHI |
| 55.39 | 6 | 41 | yzFGIJ |
| 55.38 | 6 | 42 | yzFGIJ |
| 55.37 | 4 | 36 | yzFJ |
| 55.36 | 5 | 40 | OzFJK |
| 55.35 | 5 | 30 | yzFJK |
| 55.34 | 2 | 11 | yK |
| 55.33 | 3 | 10 | yJX |
| 55.32 | 2 | 13 | yJ |
| 55.31 | 2 | 8 | yJ |

**10-23 Micro Analysis:** The higher opening, the wide initial balance and the early structure of this day (Y single TPOs from 5540 to 5552, with Z eliminating the possibility of a Y period selling extreme) indicate an **early** buying imbalance. This signals the possibility/probability of directional buying that will keep the bull market intact. Note that the market probes lower in B period, testing the Z low. Upon exhausting the selling without eradicating the single TPOs, but discovering a defined buying imbalance, price extends up in a one timeframe mode, with the wide (i.e., facilitating) ranges at each half hour through H scoring higher lows and higher or equal highs. Markets usually make a sustained directional move that occurs throughout the day in this (single dominant other timeframe group) manner. Note the double distribution trend day structure, indicative of buying supporting the market at higher levels.

**10-23 Macro Analysis:** The strong initiating buying extreme, the wide, untested single TPOs (5586-5598), combined with the day structure indicates a strong buying imbalance. The high-low range and the degree of imbalance in this buying trend day compared to the selling trend day occurring on the 21st, illustrates that buying imbalance remains dominant at this time. Also note another bull market symptom: the week finishes up well, settling near the highs of the week. The market-imposed timeframe of the week's end brings in buying — both from short covering and new and "add-on" buying. The market continues in a maturing bull phase, and over the longer term the other timeframe buying imbalance can be expected to create higher values. Keep in mind, though, that major directional trending days are generally not followed by similar-type days.

TRADING SIMULATOR - Based on the CBOT Market Profile*

DM 1287 13:20:12 56.46  O 55.58  H 56.55  L 55.40  V 1499  TB 220^41  TV 1328^125
         10/23/87

| | | | |
|---|---|---|---|
| 56.54 | 1 | 7 | H |
| 56.52 | 3 | 26 | HI |
| 56.50 | 4 | 33 | HI |
| 56.48 | 5 | 32 | HIK |
| 56.46 | 8 | 46 | HIJX |
| 56.44 | 8 | 62 | HIJK |
| 56.42 | 8 | 64 | HIJK |
| 56.40 | 9 | 52 | GHIJK |
| 56.38 | 10 | 35 | FGHIJK |
| 56.36 | 9 | 19 | FGHJK |
| 56.34 | 8 | 20 | EFGH |
| 56.32 | 8 | 38 | EFGH |
| 56.30 | 7 | 44 | EFGH |
| 56.28 | 8 | 24 | EFGH |
| 56.26 | 8 | 52 | EFGH |
| 56.24 | 8 | 73 | EFGH |
| 56.22 | 8 | 50 | EFGH |
| 56.20 | 7 | 64 | EFGH |
| 56.18 | 6 | 43 | EFG |
| 56.16 | 5 | 18 | EFG |
| 56.14 | 4 | 21 | EFG |
| 56.12 | 4 | 13 | EFG |
| 56.10 | 4 | 19 | EFG |
| 56.08 | 4 | 20 | EF |
| 56.06 | 2 | 12 | F |
| 56.04 | 3 | 11 | EFG |
| 56.02 | 2 | 3 | E |
| 56.00 | 4 | 10 | EF |
| 55.98 | 2 | 3 | E |
| 55.96 | 2 | 10 - | E |
| 55.94 | 2 | 22 | E |
| 55.92 | 2 | 18 | E |
| 55.90 | 2 | 12 | E |
| 55.88 | 2 | 5 | E |
| 55.86 | 2 | 3 | D |
| 55.84 | 4 | 9 | DE |
| 55.82 | 3 | 20 | DE |
| 55.80 | 4 | 17 | DE |
| 55.78 | 4 | 17 | DE |
| 55.76 | 3 | 6 | DE |
| 55.74 | 3 | 5 | CD |
| 55.72 | 4 | 18 | CD |
| 55.70 | 6 | 24 | ACD |
| 55.68 | 6 | 33 | ACD |
| 55.66 | 6 | 33 | ACD |
| 55.64 | 10 | 50 | yzABCD |
| 55.62 | 10 | 47 | yzABC |
| 55.60 | 10 | 60 | yzABC |
| 55.58 | 7 | 84 | OzBC |
| 55.56 | 5 | 51 | yzB |
| 55.54 | 4 | 19 | yB |
| 55.52 | 2 | 4 | y |
| 55.50 | 2 | 4 | y |
| 55.48 | 1 | 1 | y |
| 55.46 | 2 | 3 | y |
| 55.44 | 2 | 3 | y |
| 55.42 | 1 | 1 | y |
| 55.40 | 1 | 1 | y |

Weekly Bar Chart
Week of 10-23-87

*CBOT Market Profile and Market Profile are registered trademarks of the
Chicago Board of Trade
Copyright Board of Trade of the City of Chicago 1984. All Rights Reserved.

**10-26 Micro Analysis**: A quieter day with higher values develops out of an undistinguished initial balance, and price probes in both directions fail to continue. Note that this rest day nevertheless records significantly higher value and settles above Friday's highs.

**10-26 Macro Analysis**: This day would be termed a continuation day, even though it is higher, balanced and facilitated less trade. This is due to the fact that when one of the two other timeframe groups is operating at its highest level of activity, as is the case in the previous session, a quiet market which allows a regrouping can be expected. This is what occurs, and the higher values indicate that while "resting," buyers are still a force in the market. As surmised, sellers are on the defensive, otherwise this day would have provided values lower than it did. If the market is going to continue to trend higher, it can now do so, having rested and set back.

TRADING SIMULATOR - Based on the CBOT Market Profile*

DM 1287 13:20:02 56.55   O 56.68   H 56.78   L 56.49   V   893 TB 61^88   TV 313^512
              10/26/87

```
56.78     0     0
56.77     1     5   C
56.76     1     8   C
56.75     1    17   C
56.74     1    15   C
56.73     2    10   CG
56.72     3    12   yCG
56.71     3    14   yCG
56.70     4    22   yzCG
56.69     5    30   yzACG
56.68     7    47   OzACDGJ
56.67     8    65   yzACDGIJ
56.66     9    65   yzABCDGIJ
56.65     9  + 68   yzABCDGIJ
56.64    11    60   yzABCDFGHIJ
56.63  + 11    58 - yzABCDFGHIJ
56.62    10    51   yzABCDFHIJ
56.61     8    41   yzBCFHIJ
56.60     8    43   yzBDFHIJ
56.59     8    42   yzBDFHIJ
56.58     8    40   yzBDFHIJ
56.57     9    42   yzBDEFHIJ
56.56     9    37   yzBDEFHIJ
56.55     8    26   yzDEFIJX
56.54     6    24   yzDEJK
56.53     4    21   DEJK
56.52     4    14   DEJK
56.51     4     8   DEJK
56.50     2     4   EJ
56.49     1     1   E
```

**10-27 Micro Analysis**: After a quiet initial balance and a subsequent quiet hour testing both ends of the day's range, this day is shaping up either to be another rest day or a directional day. This quietness is the ideal type of opening from which a directional move can be sustained. After the C period extends with such velocity following what was quiet trading within the initial balance, the opening at 5661 looks like it may be the low for the day, another very bullish signal. Again, a one timeframe move develops. The market indicates the degree of imbalance (and, hence, strength) by the wide number of untested single TPOs in both C and E periods.

**10-27 Macro Analysis**: This continued strength after the rest day is to be expected. Price moving higher over time, creating new highs on the move, is caused by nothing more than the continued buying imbalance. Note that the buying that caused the imbalance on the day was in retrospect evident early as illustrated by the opening being the day's low.

TRADING SIMULATOR - Based on the CBOT Market Profile*

DM 1287 13:19:30 57.08  O 56.61  H 57.26  L 56.61  V 1107 TB 48^112 TV 453^618
             10/27/87

```
57.26     0      0
57.25     1      3    G
57.24     1      2    G
57.23     1      3    G
57.22     1      5    G
57.21     2      8    GH
57.20     3     12    GHI
57.19     3     16    GHI
57.18     3     22    GHI
57.17     3     27    GHI
57.16     3     29    GHI
57.15     3     24    GHI
57.14     3     23    GHI
57.13     3     27    GHI
57.12     3     33    GHI
57.11     3     29    GHI
57.10     3     21    GHI
57.09     4     19    GHIK
57.08     5     24    GHIJX
57.07     4     30    GIJK
57.06 ┼   6     33    EFGIJK
57.05     5     31    EFGIJ
57.04     5     30    EFGIJ
57.03     4     36 ┼  EFIJ
57.02     4     31    EFIJ
57.01     4     25    EFIJ
57.00     4     29    EFIJ
56.99     4     34    EFIJ
56.98     4     26    EFIJ
56.97     4     23    EFIJ
56.96     2     23    EF
56.95     2     14    EF
56.94     2      8    EF
56.93     2      7  - EF
56.92     1      3    E
56.91     1      1    E
56.90     0      0
56.89     1      2    E
56.88     1      4    E
56.87     1      4    E
56.86     1      7    E
56.85     2      9    DE
56.84     2     11    DE
56.83     2     16    DE
56.82     2     17    DE
56.81     2     19    CD
56.80     2     19    CD
56.79     2     12    CD
56.78     2     13    CD
56.77     2     12    CD
56.76     1      4    C
56.75     1      1    C
56.74     1      3    C
56.73     1      3    C
56.72     1      4    C
56.71     2     12    yC
56.70     4     24    yzBC
56.69     4     28    yzBC
56.68     4     25    yzBC
56.67     4     28    yzAB
56.66     4     32    yzAB
56.65     4     21    yzAB
56.64     3     22    yAB
56.63     3     27    yAB
56.62     3     13    yAB
56.61     2      2    OB
```

**10-28 Micro Analysis**: Opening higher at 5728, the market sets up during the initial balance in much the same manner as the 23rd. Yet A period does not range extend up. The early part of the day is spent probing low — making a single tick low in B period that does not follow through — and then probing high by a single TPO in D, and then down again in E. But the velocity comes in G period, as the dominant group, the other timeframe buyers, continue to exert themselves. Higher lows and higher highs from G through J periods signal the imbalance that pulls values higher.

**10-28 Macro Analysis**: In light of the recent tremendous buying imbalance, the early selling range extensions
that fail would not be of concern, particularly since developing value is sharply higher than the previous day and prices find support at the previous session highs. G period's price probe up that is not met with any selling indicates that these higher prices are not successfully attracting other timeframe selling. Rather, subsequent higher prices bring in more buying, symptomatic of a mature bull move. These last several days illustrate clearly that a) the trend (imbalance caused by the dominant other timeframe group) is your friend, b) imbalance (illustrated through this logical approach) causes the trend and therefore must exist in a readable form **early** in the trend (see A period, 10-22 through end of day 11-02) and lastly, c) the degree to which the imbalance (trend) will continue to unfold is a function of the degree and progression of the present imbalance, which can be measured both in terms of its velocity and maturity.

TRADING SIMULATOR - Based on the CBOT Market Profile*

DM 1287 13:20:04 57.88  O 57.28  H 58.07  L 57.24  V 1480 TB 166ˆ46 TV 1084ˆ313
         10/28/87

| | | | |
|---|---|---|---|
| 58.06 | 1 | 3 | J |
| 58.04 | 2 | 13 | J |
| 58.02 | 2 | 11 | J |
| 58.00 | 3 | 14 | IJ |
| 57.98 | 4 | 24 | IJ |
| 57.96 | 6 | 49 | IJK |
| 57.94 | 6 | 48 | IJK |
| 57.92 | 6 | 69 | IJK |
| 57.90 | 8 | 72 | HIJK |
| 57.88 | 8 | 54 | HIJX |
| 57.86 | 8 | 43 | HIJK |
| 57.84 | 8 | 39 | HIJK |
| 57.82 | 6 | 15 | HIK |
| 57.80 | 5 | 11 | HIK |
| 57.78 | 2 | 16 | H |
| 57.76 | 3 | 24 | HK |
| 57.74 | 3 | 25 | HK |
| 57.72 | 3 | 12 | HK |
| 57.70 | 3 | 15 | HK |
| 57.68 | 2 | 15 | H |
| 57.66 | 2 | 18 | H |
| 57.64 | 3 | 13 - | HK |
| 57.62 | 2 | 4 | H |
| 57.60 | 3 | 7 | HK |
| 57.58 | 3 | 5 | GH |
| 57.56 | 2 | 5 | G |
| 57.54 | 2 | 6 | G |
| 57.52 | 2 | 7 | G |
| 57.50 | 2 | 3 | G |
| 57.48 | 2 | 2 | G |
| 57.46 | 4 | 9 | zDG |
| 57.44 | 6 | 33 | zDG |
| 57.42 | 8 | 43 | zCDG |
| 57.40 | 9 | 46 | yzCDG |
| 57.38 | 11 | 68 | yzCDEG |
| 57.36 | 14 | 91 | yzACDEG |
| 57.34 | 17 | 151 | yzABCDEFG |
| 57.32 | 17 + 154 | | yzABCDEFG |
| 57.30 | 12 | 134 | yzABEFG |
| 57.28 | 10 | 77 | OABEF |
| 57.26 | 7 | 25 | yBEF |
| 57.24 | 2 | 6 | E |

**10-29 Micro Analysis:** The open is slightly higher than the close of the previous session and the initial balance leaves a selling extreme. In A period, however, buyers push the market two ticks above the initial balance. This other time-frame buying activity continues upward in B, more than doubling the initial balance. Sellers take advantage of these prices and move the market lower in a one timeframe fashion through J. J period extends below the day's lows, which triggers other timeframe buying. The market closes in the middle of the initial balance.

**10-29 Macro Analysis:** Volatility marks the day. The low of the day moves to the low of the previous session's higher distribution. It is apparent and understandable at these high prices that selling has finally entered and the other timeframe buyers and other timeframe sellers are in a tug-of-war. But judging by the range extensions, the buyers are still able to create more imbalance, preventing one from selling this market yet. Expect Friday to be strong; if the bull market this week concludes as is typical of a mature bull market (prices moving higher over time) this market should culminate with a strong close on the week.

TRADING SIMULATOR - Based on the CBOT Market Profile*

DM 1287 13:20:06 57.88  O 57.93  H 58.33  L 57.80  V 1405  TB 102^102TV 1147^203
          10/29/87

```
58.33   0    0
58.32   1    2    B
58.31   1    2    B
58.30   2    8    BC
58.29   2   13    BC
58.28   2   24    BC
58.27   2   28    BC
58.26   2   18    BC
58.25   2   12    BC
58.24   2   12    BC
58.23   3   12    BCE
58.22   3   17    BCE
58.21   2   21    BC
58.20   3   30    BCE
58.19   5   48    BCDEF
58.18   5   51    BCDEF
58.17   5   38    BCDEF
58.16   5   33    BCDEF
58.15   5   46    BCDEF
58.14   5   42    BCDEF
58.13   4   26    BDEF
58.12   7   32    BCDEFGH
58.11   6   41    BDEFGH
58.10   7   41    BCDEFGH
58.09   6   38    BDEFGH
58.08   7   39    BCDEFGH
58.07   5   35    BEFGH
58.06   5   35  - BEFGH
58.05   7   32    BCEFGHI
58.04   6   32    BEFGHI
58.03   7   35    ABEFGHI
58.02   6   31    ABFGHI
58.01   5   31    yAGHI
58.00   5   34    yAGHI
57.99   5   38    yAGHI
57.98   5   36    yAGIJ
57.97   6   24    yzAGIJ
57.96   6   31    yzAGIJ
57.95   6   38    yzAGIJ
57.94   6   40    yzAGIJ
57.93   6   55    OzAGIJ
57.92   7   50    yzAGIJK
57.91   7   34    yzAGIJK
57.90   6   28    yzAGJK
57.89   5   27    yzGJK
57.88   5   25    yzGJX
57.87   3   12    yzJ
57.86   1    8    J
57.85   1    7    J
57.84   1    4    J
57.83   1    3    J
57.82   1    2    J
57.81   1    2    J
57.80   1    1    J
```

**10-30 Micro**: The open is 11 ticks lower than the close on 10-29, and immediate responsive buying comes into the market at these perceived low prices, forming a responsive buying extreme. Note that the opening is only three ticks off the low. Z period moves a bit higher than the previous day's close as the initial balance sets up. A, B, and C periods move successively higher, signaling that the other timeframe buyer is active at these prices. Continuation is indicated. The market then builds value on the high end of the previous day's value area, closes in the upper third of the day's range, and settles the week near the top of the week's range — price moving higher through time.

**10-30 Macro**: By structure alone (ignoring how it unfolded over time), this day's profile resembles 10-20. However, instead of falling and bouncing back as it did then, this market finds buying imbalance almost from the opening. For four days in a row the buying range extensions have been significantly more pronounced and directional than the selling range extensions. This is a market that does not offer the seller any time with which to wait for the market to break, unless the sale is positioned at price far above value. Because this market is so dramatically imbalanced, it can be expected to move directionally.

TRADING SIMULATOR - Based on the CBOT Market Profile*

DM 1287 13:20:22 58.10  O 57.77  H 58.29  L 57.74  V  997 TB 74^87  TV 381^556
            10/30/87

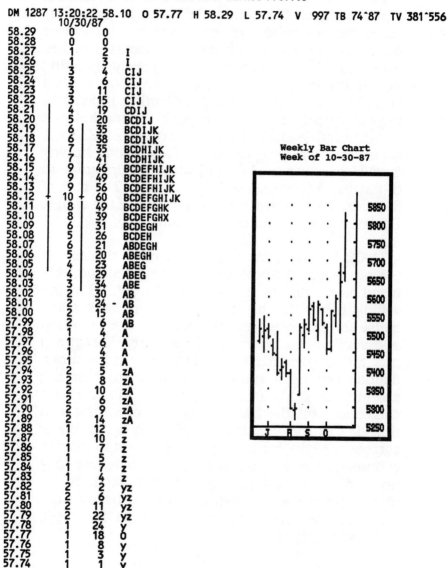

| 58.29 | 0 | 0 | |
|---|---|---|---|
| 58.28 | 0 | 0 | |
| 58.27 | 1 | 2 | I |
| 58.26 | 1 | 3 | I |
| 58.25 | 3 | 4 | CIJ |
| 58.24 | 3 | 6 | CIJ |
| 58.23 | 3 | 11 | CIJ |
| 58.22 | 3 | 15 | CIJ |
| 58.21 | 4 | 19 | CDIJ |
| 58.20 | 5 | 20 | BCDIJ |
| 58.19 | 6 | 35 | BCDIJK |
| 58.18 | 6 | 38 | BCDIJK |
| 58.17 | 7 | 35 | BCDHIJK |
| 58.16 | 7 | 41 | BCDHIJK |
| 58.15 | 9 | 46 | BCDEFHIJK |
| 58.14 | 9 | 49 | BCDEFHIJK |
| 58.13 | 9 | 56 | BCDEFHIJK |
| 58.12 | 10 | 60 | BCDEFGHIJK |
| 58.11 | 8 | 49 | BCDEFGHK |
| 58.10 | 8 | 39 | BCDEFGHX |
| 58.09 | 6 | 31 | BCDEGH |
| 58.08 | 5 | 26 | BCDEH |
| 58.07 | 6 | 21 | ABDEGH |
| 58.06 | 5 | 20 | ABEGH |
| 58.05 | 4 | 23 | ABEG |
| 58.04 | 4 | 29 | ABEG |
| 58.03 | 3 | 34 | ABE |
| 58.02 | 2 | 30 | AB |
| 58.01 | 2 | 24 | AB |
| 58.00 | 2 | 15 | AB |
| 57.99 | 2 | 6 | AB |
| 57.98 | 1 | 4 | A |
| 57.97 | 1 | 6 | A |
| 57.96 | 1 | 4 | A |
| 57.95 | 1 | 3 | A |
| 57.94 | 2 | 5 | zA |
| 57.93 | 2 | 8 | zA |
| 57.92 | 2 | 10 | zA |
| 57.91 | 2 | 6 | zA |
| 57.90 | 2 | 9 | zA |
| 57.89 | 2 | 14 | zA |
| 57.88 | 1 | 12 | z |
| 57.87 | 1 | 10 | z |
| 57.86 | 1 | 7 | z |
| 57.85 | 1 | 5 | z |
| 57.84 | 1 | 7 | z |
| 57.83 | 1 | 4 | z |
| 57.82 | 2 | 2 | yz |
| 57.81 | 2 | 6 | yz |
| 57.80 | 2 | 11 | yz |
| 57.79 | 2 | 22 | yz |
| 57.78 | 1 | 24 | y |
| 57.77 | 1 | 18 | O |
| 57.76 | 1 | 8 | y |
| 57.75 | 1 | 3 | y |
| 57.74 | 1 | 1 | y |

Weekly Bar Chart
Week of 10-30-87

**11-02 Micro**: Not surprisingly, the market opens higher. The initial balance is especially quiet, beckoning for other timeframe buyers or sellers to come into the market. Because higher prices have not attracted sellers recently, a buying directional type day can be expected from such a quiet (non-holiday) opening. The other timeframe buyers quickly move in and push the market in a one timeframe mode up. In their doing so, Z forms an initiating buying extreme. This strong buying activity persists to H period when sellers come in to form a responsive selling extreme. The rest of the day's trade hovers at the top end of the range. This day can be considered a trend day.

**11-02 Macro**: Note that in terms of the size of the range and the velocity of range extension, this trend day is not as strong as 10-23, 27, 28 or the selling trend day on 10-21. This presents some cause for concern. The market may need to chop and vacillate as other timeframe buyers regroup and gather strength. It is the fifth day in a row of a defined buying imbalance, pointing towards the assumption that the market may be in store for a correction, on the basis of a) lack of strength in this day b) the fact that markets need to either correct or rest after such a move (except in a blow-off climax, which this day's weaker structure does not indicate), and c) the fact that weak early-strong late is the bull market pattern, both on the day and the week. Strength early in the week could set up for pull-back.

TRADING SIMULATOR - Based on the CBOT Market Profile*

DM 1287 13:20:00 58.70  O 58.40  H 58.82  L 58.30  V  896  TB 34^99  TV 654^196
11/02/87

```
58.82   0    0
58.81   1    9   H
58.80   1   12   H
58.79   1   12   H
58.78   1   14   H
58.77   1   13   H
58.76   2    8   HI
58.75   2    7   HI
58.74   4   16   FHIJ
58.73   6   33   EFGHIJ
58.72   6   38   EFGHIJ
58.71   7   34   EFGHIJK
58.70   7   38   EFGHIJX
58.69   7   39   EFGHIJK
58.68   6   38   EFGHIJ
58.67   5   31   EFGIJ
58.66   3   27   EFG
58.65   3   29   EFG
58.64   3   25   EFG
58.63   3   11   EFG
58.62   2    5   EG
58.61   2    4   EG
58.60   1    6   E
58.59   1    6   E
58.58   2    6   DE
58.57   2    6   DE
58.56   2    9 - DE
58.55   2    8   DE
58.54   3    7   CDE
58.53   3   12   CDE
58.52   3   16   CDE
58.51   4   14   BCDE
58.50   3   19   BCD
58.49   3   20   BCD
58.48   3   14   BCD
58.47   3   21   BCD
58.46   3   44   BCD
58.45   4   46   ABCD
58.44   4   27   ABCD
58.43   4   19   ABCD
58.42   3   14   ACD
58.41   1    7   A
58.40   2    3   OA
58.39   2    7   yA
58.38   2   15   yA
58.37   2   21   yA
58.36   2   16   yA
58.35   3   16   yzA
58.34   3   21   yzA
58.33   2   11   yz
58.32   1    8   z
58.31   1    8   z
58.30   1    3   z
```

**11-03 Micro**: The day opens much higher than the close of the previous session and the initial balance is a bit larger, but it is still relatively quiet. Given the previous session's less than robust trend day up, we conclude that this significantly higher opening presents an opportunity for the trader probing the short side of the market. B period extends the initial balance down as the other timeframe seller acts responsively, as can be expected, reacting by selling price above the previous session's value. This strong selling activity continues through E period in a one timeframe mode. E period probes through the previous session's low by 3 ticks and bounces, forming a buying extreme. This market moves too far and too fast (70 ticks from high to low) which promotes responsive other timeframe buying to come in. The market moves higher and closes near the previous day's close.

**11-03 Macro**: Based on the breadth of the recent move, market-generated information would suggest that this day serves the same purpose as 10-20, namely to shake weak longs off of a strong bull trend. We are not surprised at the fact that sellers dominate at this time, given the somewhat lackluster buying imbalance of the previous session. Note that counter trend pullbacks are often more furious and directional than the primary trend. Having shaken out weak longs, if the market is still strong, it will need to work higher. Due to the level of other timeframe activity on this very big day, the market may need to rest.

TRADING SIMULATOR - Based on the CBOT Market Profile*

DM 1287 13:19:59 58.59  O 58.96  H 59.04  L 58.27  V 1323 TB 119˜80 TV 834˜437
         11/03/87

```
59.04     0     0
59.02     4    17     yA
59.00     4    68     yA
58.98     7    59     yzAB
58.96     8    61     OzAB
58.94     7    54     yzAB
58.92     4    26     zB
58.90     3     9     zB
58.88     2     5     B
58.86     4    31     BC
58.84     4    28     BC
58.82     4    18     BCG
58.80     4    22     CG
58.78     4    21     CG
58.76     4    32     CG
58.74     4    30     CG
58.72     5    30     CFG
58.70     6    31     CFG
58.68     9    60     CFGHI
58.66    10    55     CFGHI
58.64    11    51   - CDFGHI
58.62    11    57     CDEFHI
58.60    13    68     CDEFHIJ
58.58    14    96     DEFHIJX
58.56    12    70     DEFHJK
58.54     9    41     DEFJK
58.52     7    45     DEFJ
58.50     7    40     DEFJ
58.48     4    32     DE
58.46     4    35     DE
58.44     4    12     DE
58.42     3     7     DE
58.40     4    20     DE
58.38     4    36     DE
58.36     3    13     DE
58.34     2    10     E
58.32     2     6     E
58.30     2    12     E
58.28     2    12     E
```

**11-04 Micro**: Opening higher, the market moves higher and then lower in forming a wide initial balance. A period probes lower, forming a buying extreme as B moves higher than A. The

market facilitates trade the rest of the day in the initial balance area. After I period forms a selling extreme of two ticks, the day trades and then settles in the high end of value.

**11-04 Macro**: Experiencing two selling days in a row, a weaker market should have extended the selling reaction further, forcing price lower. An endless ebb and flow between buyers and sellers, the market exhibits a strong bounce during this and the previous trading session. This bounce indicates that selling dominance may be about expended. If so, the market is set to move higher. A lower opening should be a buying opportunity.

TRADING SIMULATOR - Based on the CBOT Market Profile*

DM 1287 13:20:01 58.83  O 58.75  H 58.92  L 58.45  V 1142 TB 108ˆ83 TV 318ˆ762
         11/04/87

```
58.92     0     0
58.91     1     1   I
58.90     1     2   I
58.89     2     7   yI
58.88     2    15   yI
58.87     2    15   yI
58.86     3    12   yIK
58.85     4    19   yzIK
58.84     5    30   yzIJK
58.83     5    26   yzIJX
58.82     7    26   yzDHIJK
58.81     6    31   yzDHIJ
58.80     6    35   yzDHIJ
58.79     6    42   yzDHIJ
58.78     6    56   yzDHIJ
58.77     6 ┌  62   yzDHIJ
58.76     6    53   yzDHIJ
58.75     7    46   OzDEHIJ
58.74     5    34   zDEHI
58.73     4    20   zDHI
58.72     3    16   zDH
58.71     5    16   zDEFH
58.70     6    17   zDEFGH
58.69     6    18   zDEFGH
58.68     6    24  - zDEFGH
58.67     8    36   zBCDEFGH
58.66     7    40   zBCEFGH
58.65     8    31   zBCDEFGH
58.64     7    31   zBCDEFG
58.63     7    36   zBCDEFG
58.62     8    37   zABCDEFG
58.61     8    36   zABCDEFG
58.60     8    38   zABCDEFG
58.59     6    41   zABCFG
58.58     5    38   zABCF
58.57     3    35   ABC
58.56     2    27   AB
58.55     2    15   AB
58.54     2    10   AB
58.53     2     8   AB
58.52     2     8   AB
58.51     2    12   AB
58.50     2    12   AB
58.49     2     9   AB
58.48     1     8   A
58.47     1     5   A
58.46     1     3   A
58.45     1     2   A
```

*CBOT Market Profile and Market Profile are registered trademarks of the
Chicago Board of Trade
Copyright Board of Trade of the City of Chicago 1984.  All Rights Reserved.

**11-05 Micro**: Again, the market opens higher.
This day has a much quieter initial balance than
on 11-04, hinting that any imbalance may force
the market directionally in a sustained manner.
The other timeframe buyer is quiet until the C
period when the range is extended up five ticks.
Each higher half hour has a broader range which
indicates facilitation of trade at higher prices. This
strong activity continues through F period, which
forms a responsive selling extreme. The activity
for the rest of the day is in the top half of the day's
range.

**11-05 Macro**: By the close of this day, the market has moved significantly from last week's settlement and has a 200 point high-low range on the
week. Strong buying emerges on this day, which,
combined with a defined responsive selling
extreme, raises the chance of a selling reaction
developing. Clearly, the long-term bull market
marches on, though the market may need to rest
and regroup for some time. Tomorrow's session
can be expected to close in top quarter to one-fifth
of the week's high/low range.

TRADING SIMULATOR - Based on the CBOT Market Profile*

```
DM 1287 13:20:01 59.81  O 59.17  H 60.26  L 59.08  V 1887 TB 64^198 TV 541^1279
         11/05/87
60.26      0     0
60.24      2     2    F
60.22      2     2    F
60.20      2     4    F
60.18      2    13    F
60.16      2    12    F
60.14      2    24    F
60.12      2    26    F
60.10      2    18    F
60.08      2    30    F
60.06      2    21    F
60.04      4    11    FGI
60.02      6    22    FGI
60.00      7    20    EFGI
59.98      9    48    EFGHI
59.96     10    67    EFGHI
59.94     12    72    EFGHIJ
59.92     11    90    EFGHIJ
59.90     12   125    EFGHIJ
59.88      9    81    EGHIJK
59.86     10    58    EGHJK
59.84     10    57    EGHJK
59.82      9    34    EGHJK
59.80      6    26    EGJX
59.78      4    19    EG
59.76      4    11    EG
59.74      6    16    DEG
59.72      6    18    DEG
59.70      6    24    DEG
59.68      4    30    DE
59.66      4    38  - DE
59.64      4    52    DE
59.62      4    26    DE
59.60      4    10    DE
59.58      4    16    DE
59.56      3    20    DE
59.54      2    25    D
59.52      2    35    D
59.50      2    21    D
59.48      2    26    D
59.46      2     6    D
59.44      2     8    D
59.42      4     8    CD
59.40      4    15    CD
59.38      4    16    CD
59.36      4    14    CD
59.34      2    12    C
59.32      3    14    zC
59.30      4    21    zC
59.28      5    34    zAC
59.26      6    97    zAC
59.24      6    76    zAC
59.22      7    46    zABC
59.20      9    43    yzABC
59.18      7    43    yzAB
59.16      6    63    OzB
59.14      6    55    yzB
59.12      6    35    yzB
59.10      4    22    yB
59.08      3     8    yB
```

**11-06 Micro**: The day opens about at the previous day's close, and the initial balance is wide.
The low is near the low of previous day's high distribution. An early initiating buying extreme is
formed in Z period. Other timeframe buying
activity comes into the market in B period and in C
period forms a responsive selling extreme. The
market facilitates trade in a two timeframe mode
for the rest of the day and closes in the middle of
the day's range.

**11-06 Macro**: A pronounced buying imbalance
persists, which, given the breadth of the recent
move, would be expected on the last trading session of only a very strong market. This is a continuation day up, given the character of the day
within the context of the week. Note that we do not
close on the absolute high of the day and week.

TRADING SIMULATOR - Based on the CBOT Market Profile*

DM 1287 13:20:02 59.88   O 59.79   H 60.18   L 59.60   V 1305 TB 109ˆ119TV 536ˆ708
              11/06/87

```
60.18     0      0
60.17     1      2     C
60.16     1      4     C
60.15     1      6     C
60.14     1      7     C
60.13     3      9     CDE
60.12     3     16     CDE
60.11     3     20     CDE
60.10     4     22     BCDE
60.09     4     15     BCDE
60.08     4     10     BCDE
60.07     4     13     BCDE
60.06     4     20     BCDE
60.05     4     26     BCDE
60.04     4     21     BCDE
60.03     5     28     BCDEJ
60.02     6     36     BCDEIJ
60.01     6     33     BCDEIJ
60.00     6     35     BCDEIJ
59.99     6     29     BCDEIJ
59.98     6     32     BCDEIJ
59.97     6     43     BCDEIJ
59.96     8     49     BCDEHIJK
59.95     8     59     BCDEHIJK
59.94     8     61     BCDFHIJK
59.93     7     55     BCFHIJK
59.92     8     48     BCEFHIJK
59.91     7     32     BFGHIJK
59.90     7     36     BEFGHJK
59.89     6     27   - BFGHJK
59.88     6     27     BEFGHX
59.87     5     23     yBFGH
59.86     6     30     yBEFGH
59.85     5     30     yBEFG
59.84     5     12     yBEFG
59.83     5     16     yBEFG
59.82     5     21     yBEFG
59.81     4     18     yBEF
59.80     4     29     yBEF
59.79     4     29     OBEF
59.78     5     17     yzABF
59.77     4     14     yABF
59.76     5     11     yzABF
59.75     5      7     yzABF
59.74     3      6     yzA
59.73     3     11     yzA
59.72     3     16     yzA
59.71     2     22     zA
59.70     3     26     yzA
59.69     2     21     zA
59.68     3     27     yzA
59.67     2     25     zA
59.66     2     16     zA
59.65     3     15     yzA
59.64     2     15     zA
59.63     3     15     yzA
59.62     1      7     z
59.61     1      3     z
59.60     1      1     z
```

Weekly Bar Chart
Week of 11-06-87

**11-09 Micro**: The market opens higher. The initial balance develops a good-sized range and is violated on the downside in A period by a single tick. This shows that the other timeframe seller is not willing to sell the market at these prices. The single print A is a sign of the inability to follow through. As seen before, a range extension of only a single tick will often send a market in the opposite direction. The other timeframe buyer comes in, causing imbalance. In C period, the market scores a buying range extension as the market is off to active, one timeframe activity. As G period extends upward, sellers alert to these high prices respond, and G forms a responsive selling extreme. The market facilitates trade in these higher regions for the rest of the day.

**11-09 Macro**: Note the strong early imbalance. The market opens three ticks off the low, and the dramatic single print TPOs left from 6018-22 again indicate the great degree of aggressive buying. Also note that responsive selling is again apparent, but its existence at higher prices is expected and not an indication of weakness. Again, we should be wary of strength early in a week, as noted on 11-02.

TRADING SIMULATOR - Based on the CBOT Market Profile*

DM 1287 13:19:48 60.33  O 60.02  H 60.54  L 59.99  V 1104 TB 53^105 TV 267^792
         11/09/87

```
60.54    0     0
60.53    1     6    G
60.52    1     6    G
60.51    1     5    G
60.50    1     9    G
60.49    1     9    G
60.48    2     7    FG
60.47    4    19    EFGH
60.46    5    26    EFGHI
60.45    5    25    EFGHI
60.44    5    37    EFGHI
60.43    5    42    EFGHI
60.42    5    34    EFGHI
60.41    6    39    EFGHIJ
60.40    6    45    EFGHIJ
60.39    5    36    EFHIJ
60.38    5    31    EFHIJ
60.37    6    25    EFHIJK
60.36    4    15    EIJK
60.35    5    18    DEIJK
60.34    5    21    DEIJK
60.33    3    21    DJX
60.32    2    22    DJ
60.31    2    20    DJ
60.30    2    19    DJ
60.29    3    15    CDJ
60.28    3    21    CDJ
60.27    3    25    CDJ
60.26    3    18  - CDJ
60.25    2     8    CD
60.24    2     7    CD
60.23    2     8    CD
60.22    1     6    C
60.21    1     5    C
60.20    1     5    C
60.19    1     8    C
60.18    1    10    C
60.17    2    13    zC
60.16    2    15    zC
60.15    3    21    zBC
60.14    3    29    zBC
60.13    3    27    zBC
60.12    3    23    zBC
60.11    3    21    zBC
60.10    3    19    zBC
60.09    5    23    yzABC
60.08    5    32    yzABC
60.07    4    37    yzAB
60.06    4    34    yzAB
60.05    4    30    yzAB
60.04    3    30    yAB
60.03    3    28    yAB
60.02    3    26    OAB
60.01    3    12    yAB
60.00    3     6    yAB
59.99    1     2    A
```

**11-10 Micro**: The market opens sharply higher with an average sized initial balance, compared to the previous session. Other timeframe activity does not start until C period when selling comes into the market. The longs try to stop this but these are futile attempts as shorts move the market down until G period. Responsive buying finally comes in G period, forming a very weak responsive buying extreme. The close does not indicate any strong buying on the part of the other timeframe participant as trade remains in the bottom half of the day's range.

**11-10 Macro**: Some pre-opening considerations: Given the rally of the last five sessions, plus the strength early in the week — a cautionary condition late in a bull run — the direction of the range extension on this day should be heavily weighted. A range extension up signals that other timeframe buyers remain committed and dominant, while a range extension down signals that the market has moved too far, too fast, and needs to rest. As the day unfolds, signals of weakness abound. No longer are quieter, higher, but non-facilitating openings used as opportunities to buy. The higher opening sell-off shows that sellers are attracted at higher prices. The range extension down displays aggressiveness and velocity at significantly lower prices. The range extension leaves more single print TPOs than the buying range extension of 11-09. This is a very big day in terms of high-low range — and it is a selling day. Clearly, the early in the week turnaround scenario is apparent. Note the relatively strong close, showing a two-sided market. A lower low, and a higher high, known as an "outside day," with more trade facilitation, is quite negative to any short-term bull.

TRADING SIMULATOR - Based on the CBOT Market Profile*

DM 1287 13:19:57 60.20  O 60.71  H 60.85  L 59.75  V 1738 TB 166^95 TV 135^1552
                11/10/87

```
60.84   1  |   3   z
60.82   3  |  17   zA
60.80   6  |  38   zAC
60.78   6  |  76   zAC
60.76   7 +|  96   zABC
60.74   8  |  79   zABC
60.72   8  |  33   zABC
60.70   9  |  59   OzABC
60.68   7  |  81   yzBC
60.66   7  |  52   yzBC
60.64   6  |  35   yzB
60.62   5  |  21   yzB
60.60   3  |  20   yC
60.58   4  |  23   yC
60.56   4  |  14   yC
60.54   2  |   5   C
60.52   2  |   5   C
60.50   1  |   7   C
60.48   2  |   7   C
60.46   2  |   8   C
60.44   3  |   5   CE
60.42   2  |   6   E
60.40   3  |  27   DE
60.38   7  |  43   CDEF
60.36   5  |  52   DEF
60.34   7  |  45   CDEF
60.32   6  |  33   DEF
60.30   6  |  32 - CDEF
60.28   4  |   5   DF
60.26   3  |  10   DF
60.24   4  |  35   DF
60.22   4  |  38   DF
60.20   6  |  47   DFJX
60.18   7  |  44   DFJK
60.16   8  |  54   DFGJK
60.14   9 +|  55   DFGJK
60.12   8  |  35   DFGJ
60.10   7  |  20   DFGIJ
60.08   6  |  11   GIJ
60.06   4  |  12   IJ
60.04   7  |  32   DGIJ
60.02   5  |  24   GIJ
60.00   6  |  18   DGIJ
59.98   3  |  13   GI
59.96   5  |  38   DGI
59.94   4  |  49   GI
59.92   6  |  43   GHI
59.90   6  |  56   GHI
59.88   6  |  42   GHI
59.86   6  |  25   GHI
59.84   4  |  41   GH
59.82   4  |  47   GH
59.80   4  |  17   GH
59.78   1  |   3   G
59.76   1  |   2   G
```

**11-11 Micro**: An early entry selling imbalance is immediately apparent, and the day starts with a selling initial balance of a good size. The other timeframe sellers again extend the range in A period, causing single print TPO's; strong selling activity continues in B period. The market offers no bounce in Z, A or B period, yet another sign of weakness. D period makes the last range extension down, forming a responsive buying extreme. The rest of day builds value around the low end of the day's range.

**11-11 Macro**: Note the imbalance on this day, the fact that values were lower and that the market facilitated trade. The initiating selling extreme is more pronounced than the responsive buying extreme. The market ties the previous session's low and displays little bounce. The market condition remains weak; a pronounced rally in value over the next several sessions should not be expected, but rather unchanged or lower prices.

TRADING SIMULATOR - Based on the CBOT Market Profile*

DM 1287 13:20:12 59.83  O 60.20  H 60.21  L 59.76  V  944 TB 77^41  TV 544^306
        11/11/87

```
60.21   0    0
60.20   1    7   O
60.19   1    8   y
60.18   1    9   y
60.17   1    6   y
60.16   1    3   y
60.15   1    3   y
60.14   1    5   y
60.13   2    6   yz
60.12   1    5   z
60.11   1    3   z
60.10   1    1   z
60.09   2    7   zA
60.08   2   22   zA
60.07   2   29   zA
60.06   2   22   zA
60.05   2   14   zA
60.04   2    8   zA
60.03   1   12   A
60.02   1   13   A
60.01   1   13   A
60.00   1   12   A
59.99   2    8   AB
59.98   2    8 - AB
59.97   2    4   AB
59.96   2    5   AB
59.95   3    8   ABI
59.94   3   15   ABI
59.93   4   20   ABIJ
59.92   6   25   ABCGIJ
59.91   6   27   ABCGIJ
59.90   6   37   BCGHIJ
59.89   5   43   BCGIJ
59.88   6   53   BCGHIJ
59.87   9   80   BCDEGHIJK
59.86  10   94   BCDEFGHIJK
59.85  10   67   BCDEFGHIJK
59.84   8   64   BCDEFHIK
59.83   8   64   BCDEFHIX
59.82   5   38   BDEFI
59.81   4   27   BDEF
59.80   4   21   BDEF
59.79   2   11   DE
59.78   1    8   D
59.77   1    5   D
59.76   1    1   D
```

**11-12 Micro**: This day opens lower and for the second day in a row displays significant initiating selling which develops early. A huge initial balance is formed as the market falls out of bed. Other timeframe buyers shut off the initial selling activity around the 59.00 level forming a buying extreme in F period. The market moves into a two timeframe mode the rest of the day, facilitating trade in very large swings.

**11-12 Macro**: The increased facilitation of trade, coming as it does with lower value, a strong selling extreme and selling range extension, does not come as a surprise given the degree of initiating selling imbalance seen during the previous session. This was an active day, so one can expect a rest day to follow, but based on the points mentioned in the previous sentence (in order of importance) sellers remain the dominant other timeframe group at this juncture.

TRADING SIMULATOR - Based on the CBOT Market Profile*

DM 1287 13:20:08 59.30  O 59.73  H 59.82  L 59.02  V 1723 TB 108^160TV 1186^449
        11/12/87

```
59.82    0     0
59.80    2    10    y
59.78    2     8    y
59.76    2     8    y
59.74    2     7    y
59.72    2    10    o
59.70    2    15    y
59.68    2    14    y
59.66    1     4    y
59.64    1     1    y
59.62    0     0
59.60    3     5    yE
59.58    2    11    E
59.56    2    10    E
59.54    4    21    yDE
59.52    5    20    zDE
59.50    7    24    yzDE
59.48    8    27    yzDE
59.46    8    40    yzDE
59.44    9    66    yzCDE
59.42   10    73  - yzCDE
59.40   10    69    yzCDE
59.38    8    41    yzCDE
59.36   12    60    yzBCEFJ
59.34   13    98    yzBCEFJ
59.32   17    77    yzBCEFGJK
59.30   16    64    yzBCEFGJX
59.28   15    60    yzABFGJK
59.26   16    65    yzABFGJK
59.24   13    92    yzABFGJ
59.22   15   113    zABFGHIJ
59.20   17   159    yzABFGHIJ
59.18   15   119    zABFGHIJ
59.16   16    96    zABFGHIJ
59.14   13   105    zABFGHI
59.12   11    47    zABFHI
59.10    5    23    BFH
59.08    4    35    BF
59.06    4    18    BF
59.04    2     5    F
59.02    1     1    F
```

*CBOT Market Profile and Market Profile are registered trademarks of the
Chicago Board of Trade
Copyright Board of Trade of the City of Chicago 1984.  All Rights Reserved.

**11-13 Micro**: The open is slightly lower and Z period forms an initiating buying extreme and then wraps around Y period. Other timeframe buying continues in A period. Buying range extensions are seen in C and E periods with value slowly working its way higher in a dual auction. Note the non-facilitation of trade that follows this day dominated by the other timeframe-motivated buying imbalance. Also note that the rally merely doubles the range produced during Y-Z, a weak range extension both in absolute size and as a percentage of similarly small initial balance ranges seen on recent selling days such as 11-10 and 11-11.

**11-13 Macro**: The day is a quiet, end of the week session with defined buying which, while significant relative to the day's small range, does not go far in dissipating the selling imbalance seen recently. Note that this week is strong early and corrects late in the week — a strong sign for a bull market showing maturing tendencies. On the other hand, the market did not test the lows of the previous week at 5827. A sharply higher opening on the next session could expect to receive responsive selling. But given the longer term trend and the relatively attractive levels within that trend, it would also be attractive to buy a sharply lower opening.

TRADING SIMULATOR - Based on the CBOT Market Profile*

DM 1287 13:20:10 59.34   O 59.20   H 59.44   L 59.07   V   947 TB 43^101 TV 169^728
         11/13/87

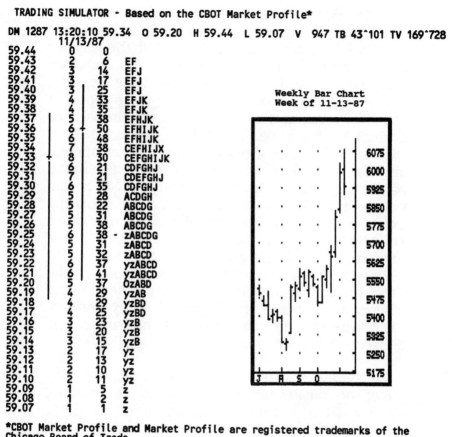

```
59.44      0      0
59.43      2      6     EF
59.42      3     14     EFJ
59.41      3     17     EFJ
59.40      3     25     EFJ
59.39      4     33     EFJK
59.38      4     35     EFJK
59.37      5     38     EFHJK
59.36      6  +  50     EFHIJK
59.35      6     48     EFHIJK
59.34      7     38     CEFHIJX
59.33      8     30     CEFGHIJK
59.32      6     21     CDFGHJ
59.31      7     21     CDEFGHJ
59.30      6     35     CDFGHJ
59.29      5     28     ACDGH
59.28      5     22     ABCDG
59.27      5     31     ABCDG
59.26      5     38     ABCDG
59.25      6     38  -  zABCDG
59.24      5     31     zABCD
59.23      5     32     zABCD
59.22      6     37     yzABCD
59.21      6     41     yzABCD
59.20      5     37     OzABD
59.19      4     29     yzAB
59.18      4     29     yzBD
59.17      4     25     yzBD
59.16      3     23     yzB
59.15      3     20     yzB
59.14      3     15     yzB
59.13      2     17     yz
59.12      2     13     yz
59.11      2     10     yz
59.10      2     11     yz
59.09      1      5     z
59.08      1      2     z
59.07      1      1     z
```

Weekly Bar Chart
Week of 11-13-87

**11-16 Micro**: The single tick range extension rule fails here. Nonetheless, two early indicators of strength that might have prevented the shorter term traders from selling were a) the fact that price was sharply lower than Friday's session, advertising for buying and nearing the support of the 5827 level, and b) the early buying imbalance evident by the time A and then B extended, at which point it was clear that the market opened only five ticks above the then-low price. The initial balance indicates buying activity as Z period wraps around Y to the upside leaving a buying extreme. A, B, and C periods all making new highs indicate more other timeframe buying. E and F periods move higher still with F leaving a large selling extreme. The other timeframe sellers take these prices to heart and drive the market back to where most of the buying begins. The day closes in the middle of the range, indicating no true winner between the other timeframe buyer and seller.

**11-16 Macro**: This day presents a prime example of the market moving too far too fast, making the situation fair in the short term. At these sharply lower prices, buyers are able to enter at advantageous prices while sellers are severely disadvantaged. Another point illustrated on this day is that the market-generated reference points referred to throughout the text not only provide current information regarding imbalance, but, as in the case of a week's high and low, can offer price areas providing expected support and resistance. This day's opening comes down near to the lows made on 11-03, where the market had encountered responsive buying which then developed into strong initiating buying activity.

TRADING SIMULATOR - Based on the CBOT Market Profile*

DM 1287 13:19:58 58.55  O 58.40  H 58.88  L 58.35  V 1173 TB 126ˆ40 TV 768ˆ342
        11/16/87

| | | | |
|---|---|---|---|
| 58.88 | 0 | 0 | |
| 58.87 | 1 | 5 | F |
| 58.86 | 1 | 8 | F |
| 58.85 | 1 | 11 | F |
| 58.84 | 1 | 12 | F |
| 58.83 | 1 | 9 | F |
| 58.82 | 1 | 5 | F |
| 58.81 | 1 | 5 | F |
| 58.80 | 1 | 7 | F |
| 58.79 | 1 | 8 | F |
| 58.78 | 1 | 10 | F |
| 58.77 | 3 | 13 | FGH |
| 58.76 | 3 | 19 | FGH |
| 58.75 | 3 | 22 | FGH |
| 58.74 | 5 | 29 | EFGHI |
| 58.73 | 5 | 41 | EFGHI |
| 58.72 | 5 | 33 | EFGHI |
| 58.71 | 4 | 19 | EGHI |
| 58.70 | 4 | 17 | EGHI |
| 58.69 | 4 | 14 | EGHI |
| 58.68 | 3 | 12 | EGI |
| 58.67 | 3 | 6 | EGI |
| 58.66 | 3 | 3 | EGI |
| 58.65 | 2 | 4 | EI |
| 58.64 | 2 | 4 | EI |
| 58.63 | 3 | 8 | CEI |
| 58.62 | 3 | 8 | CEI |
| 58.61 | 4 | 13 - | BCEI |
| 58.60 | 4 | 18 | BCEI |
| 58.59 | 4 | 18 | BCEI |
| 58.58 | 3 | 23 | BCE |
| 58.57 | 4 | 22 | BCEI |
| 58.56 | 6 | 23 | BCEIJK |
| 58.55 | 6 | 27 | BCEIJX |
| 58.54 | 6 | 28 | BCEIJK |
| 58.53 | 6 | 42 | BCEIJK |
| 58.52 | 5 | 48 | BCEIJ |
| 58.51 | 7 | 51 | ABCDEIJ |
| 58.50 | 8 | 59 | zABCDEIJ |
| 58.49 | 8 | 62 | zABCDEIJ |
| 58.48 | 9 + | 63 | yzABCDEIJ |
| 58.47 | 8 | 56 | yzABCDIJ |
| 58.46 | 7 | 55 | yzABCDI |
| 58.45 | 6 | 52 | yzABCD |
| 58.44 | 6 | 42 | yzABCD |
| 58.43 | 4 | 28 | yzAD |
| 58.42 | 4 | 22 | yzAD |
| 58.41 | 3 | 24 | yzD |
| 58.40 | 2 | 24 | Oz |
| 58.39 | 1 | 18 | y |
| 58.38 | 1 | 14 | y |
| 58.37 | 1 | 6 | y |
| 58.36 | 0 | 0 | |
| 58.35 | 1 | 1 | y |

**11-17 Micro**: The market opens a half point higher, nullifying the importance of the previous day's sharply lower opening by making 11-16 an excess day. The initial balance is normal sized and A period takes out the top of the initial balance by one tick. The market facilitates trade within the initial balance the rest of the day except during E period, which extends the initial balance downward by 3 ticks. However, other timeframe buyers quickly come in to form a buying extreme.

**11-17 Macro**: A quiet, non-facilitating session which moves the market away from support: there is little else to deduce from this day's activity. Note the A period range extension failure which then tests the low end in E. The market is resting and can now sustain a move. The question is whether buying or selling will dominate early in the next session. While a rally off of support portends for bullishness, we need to see strength early in the next session. We need to keep in mind that in a bull market, where price is moving higher over time, low prices early in the week bode well for continuation up. So far, this is exactly what is shaping up during this week.

TRADING SIMULATOR - Based on the CBOT Market Profile*

DM 1287 13:20:01 59.23  O 59.07  H 59.27  L 59.04  V  847 TB 75°53  TV 320°435
          11/17/87
```
59.27      0     0
59.26      1     4    A
59.25      3    12    zAK
59.24      5    20    yzAJK
59.23      7    37    yzABFJX
59.22      9    45    yzABDFGJK
59.21      9    50    yzABDFGJK
59.20      9    71    yzABDFGHJ
59.19      9    80    yzABDFGHJ
59.18     12    92    yzABCDEFGHIJ
59.17     12    90    yzABCDEFGHIJ
59.16     12    71    yzABCDEFGHIJ
59.15     11    52  - yzABCDEFGIJ
59.14      8    41    yzBCEFGI
59.13      7    42    yBCEFGI
59.12      7    32    yBCEFGI
59.11      6    31    yBCEFG
59.10      6    25    yBCEFG
59.09      4    17    yCEF
59.08      2    15    yE
59.07      2    11    OE
59.06      1     3    E
59.05      1     3    E
59.04      1     2    E
```

*CBOT Market Profile and Market Profile are registered trademarks of the
Chicago Board of Trade
Copyright Board of Trade of the City of Chicago 1984.  All Rights Reserved.

**11-18 Micro**: The opening is slightly lower with another normal sized initial balance. The first sign of other timeframe activity is in A period. Buyers push the market upward through B period, but selling enters in C period and the market tests the lows of the initial balance. At this point, we might expect another rest day. Failing new lows, other timeframe buyers then take control for good and easily move the market higher. There is no sign of selling until G period forms a responsive selling extreme. The market trades in the top third of the range the rest of the day. The day structure is a double distribution trend day.

**11-18 Macro**: The lower opening (which is more attractive to buyers than sellers), the C down probe failure, and the strong D period move up all spell strength and signal the renewed up auction. The abundance of single print TPOs (5921-35) also shows big anxious other timeframe buying. Because the market has rested, it can be assumed that the bull market underway will continue.

TRADING SIMULATOR - Based on the CBOT Market Profile*

DM 1287 13:20:08 59.47  O 59.04  H 59.66  L 58.95  V 1247 TB 50^122 TV 374^812
          11/18/87

| | | | |
|---|---|---|---|
| 59.66 | 0 | 0 | |
| 59.64 | 2 | 11 | G |
| 59.62 | 2 | 18 | G |
| 59.60 | 2 | 23 | G |
| 59.58 | 3 | 37 | GH |
| 59.56 | 5 | 45 | GHI |
| 59.54 | 7 | 32 | EGHI |
| 59.52 | 10 | 58 | EGHIJ |
| 59.50 | 12 | 94 | EFGHIJK |
| 59.48 | 14 | 116 | EFGHIJK |
| 59.46 | 12 | 89 | EFGHIJX |
| 59.44 | 8 | 51 | EFGHJ |
| 59.42 | 4 | 39 | EF |
| 59.40 | 4 | 31 | EF |
| 59.38 | 4 | 24 | EF |
| 59.36 | 4 | 13 | EF |
| 59.34 | 2 | 4 | E |
| 59.32 | 1 | 2 | E |
| 59.30 | 1 | 1 | E |
| 59.28 | 2 | 3 | DE |
| 59.26 | 2 | 5 | D |
| 59.24 | 2 | 5 | D |
| 59.22 | 2 | 22 | D |
| 59.20 | 3 | 21 | BD |
| 59.18 | 4 | 13 | BD |
| 59.16 | 4 | 25 | BD |
| 59.14 | 4 | 21 | BD |
| 59.12 | 6 | 41 | ABD |
| 59.10 | 7 | 46 | zABD |
| 59.08 | 9 | 65 | zABCD |
| 59.06 | 10 | 96 | yzACD |
| 59.04 | 9 | 49 | OzACD |
| 59.02 | 6 | 41 | yCD |
| 59.00 | 6 | 49 | yCD |
| 58.98 | 6 | 35 | yCD |
| 58.96 | 5 | 18 | yCD |

**11-19 Micro**: Opening higher, the market is pushed lower by initiating sellers. D period forms a large initiating buying extreme as other time-frame buyers defend their positions of yesterday. The rest of the day's trade moves into the middle of the range where it trades in a two timeframe mode.

**11-19 Macro**: A smaller version of 10-20, this day's break and subsequent bounce display pre-sumably nervous longs who are being shaken out of the market and strong other timeframe buying. Note that the market again finds buyers and bounces when probing the low of the previous day's higher distribution. One slightly negative sign is the fact that the opening is only three ticks off the high, meaning that buyers are not willing to initiate at substantially higher prices two days in a row. Perhaps this tempers the bullish expecta-tions mentioned in the last line of 11-18's macro analysis.

TRADING SIMULATOR - Based on the CBOT Market Profile*

DM 1287 13:20:16 59.64  O 59.74  H 59.77  L 59.38  V  945 TB 78^45  TV 461^413
11/19/87

```
59.77     0     0
59.76     2    17   yz
59.75     2    21   yz
59.74     2    23   Oz
59.73     2    35   yz
59.72     2    23   yz
59.71     2     4   yz
59.70     1     6   z
59.69     3    10   zAC
59.68     4    17   zABC
59.67     6    26   zABCEF
59.66     7    32   zABCEFH
59.65     7    43   zABCEFH
59.64     8    66   ABCEFHIX
59.63     8    64   ABCEFHIK
59.62    10    69   ABCEFGHIJK
59.61    10    71   ABCEFGHIJK
59.60    10    58   ABCEFGHIJK
59.59     9    61   ABCEFGHIJ
59.58     8    61   ABCEFGIJ
59.57     7    40 - ABCEGIJ
59.56     4    21   ACEJ
59.55     3    13   CEJ
59.54     3    10   CDE
59.53     3    15   CDE
59.52     3    15   CDE
59.51     3     8   CDE
59.50     2     3   DE
59.49     1     4   D
59.48     1     8   D
59.47     1    14   D
59.46     1    14   D
59.45     1    13   D
59.44     1    13   D
59.43     1    10   D
59.42     1    11   D
59.41     1    11   D
59.40     1     6   D
59.39     1     3   D
59.38     1     1   D
```

**11-20 Micro**: This day opens higher with a larger than normal sized initial balance. Initiating buying comes into the market early as other time-frame buyers move A period ten ticks above the initial balance. The buying dries up, however, and B period can only match the top that A has put in. (Above 6030, this is not surprising given the lack of initiating buyers from the previous session, more than 50 points lower.) Sellers, motivated by price above value, take control of the market with a vengeance for the next 2 1/2 hours. The panic selling does not stop until hitting the even number, 5900, where responsive buyers come in to rotate the market back up (as they did in the previous session) forming a 16 tick buying extreme. Buyers then push the market back to a bit above the middle of the range and the market closes where the sellers originally took control. Clearly, a struggle has taken place on this day.

**11-20 Macro**: A big, volatile day at the end of another big, volatile week with 200 points from low to high. Because of the volatile nature of this last day, many weaker bulls are losing confidence in the strength of the market. The paradox of a market nearing a climax phase — a phase that can last for weeks — is that the more dramatic ascent is usually preceded by an extremely volatile shaking out period. Viewed with this perspective in mind, this market still provides the market-generated guideposts necessary to expect continuation. Also, note that prices went from low to high this week, as expected in a bull market. The market also settles on the top quarter of the week's low-high range, another plus for longer term continuation. This market can still be traded from the long side.

TRADING SIMULATOR - Based on the CBOT Market Profile*

DM 1287 13:20:47 59.83  O 59.98  H 60.39  L 59.00  V 1935  TB 221ˆ97  TV 359ˆ1519
11/20/87

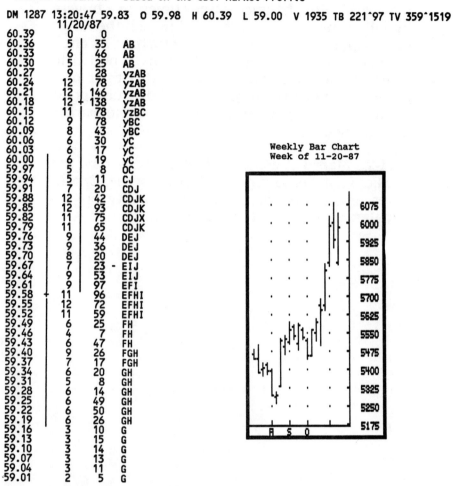

| 60.39 | 0 | 0 | |
| 60.36 | 5 | 35 | AB |
| 60.33 | 6 | 46 | AB |
| 60.30 | 5 | 25 | AB |
| 60.27 | 9 | 28 | yzAB |
| 60.24 | 12 | 78 | yzAB |
| 60.21 | 12 | 146 | yzAB |
| 60.18 | 12 | 138 | yzAB |
| 60.15 | 11 | 78 | yzBC |
| 60.12 | 9 | 78 | yBC |
| 60.09 | 8 | 43 | yBC |
| 60.06 | 6 | 30 | yC |
| 60.03 | 6 | 17 | yC |
| 60.00 | 6 | 19 | yC |
| 59.97 | 5 | 8 | OC |
| 59.94 | 5 | 11 | CJ |
| 59.91 | 7 | 20 | CDJ |
| 59.88 | 12 | 42 | CDJK |
| 59.85 | 12 | 93 | CDJK |
| 59.82 | 11 | 75 | CDJX |
| 59.79 | 11 | 65 | CDJK |
| 59.76 | 9 | 44 | DEJ |
| 59.73 | 9 | 36 | DEJ |
| 59.70 | 8 | 20 | DEJ |
| 59.67 | 7 | 23 | EIJ |
| 59.64 | 9 | 53 | EIJ |
| 59.61 | 9 | 97 | EFI |
| 59.58 | 11 | 96 | EFHI |
| 59.55 | 12 | 72 | EFHI |
| 59.52 | 11 | 59 | EFHI |
| 59.49 | 6 | 25 | FH |
| 59.46 | 4 | 7 | FH |
| 59.43 | 6 | 47 | FH |
| 59.40 | 9 | 26 | FGH |
| 59.37 | 7 | 17 | FGH |
| 59.34 | 6 | 20 | GH |
| 59.31 | 5 | 8 | GH |
| 59.28 | 6 | 14 | GH |
| 59.25 | 6 | 49 | GH |
| 59.22 | 6 | 50 | GH |
| 59.19 | 6 | 26 | GH |
| 59.16 | 3 | 10 | G |
| 59.13 | 3 | 15 | G |
| 59.10 | 3 | 14 | G |
| 59.07 | 3 | 13 | G |
| 59.04 | 3 | 11 | G |
| 59.01 | 2 | 5 | G |

Weekly Bar Chart
Week of 11-20-87

**11-23 Micro**: This day opens higher with a normal sized initial balance. Other timeframe buyers initially come in the market and extend the range up by two ticks, but fail to move it further. As often happens, sellers come in quickly in B period to offset this original extension up with their own range extension down. There is no great imbalance during the rest of the day as the market is two timeframe.

**11-23 Macro**: A consolidation, or "rest" day, the market is higher, but not facilitating trade. Expect lower prices, but also expect responsive buying imbalance (as seen lately) at those lower prices.

TRADING SIMULATOR - Based on the CBOT Market Profile*

DM 1287 13:19:53 60.04  O 60.11   H 60.16   L 59.92   V   764 TB 63^62   TV 416^292
          11/23/87
60.16        0     0
60.15        2     8    AD
60.14        2    19    AD
60.13        5    37    yzABD
60.12        6    51    yzABDF
60.11        6    43    OzABDF
60.10        7    40    yzABCDF
60.09        6    34    yzBCDF
60.08        6    21    yzBCDF
60.07        7    23    yzBCDEF
60.06        8    35    yzBCDEFH
60.05        8    49    yzBCEFGH
60.04        9    55  - yzBCEFGHX
60.03        9  + 56    yzBCEFGHK
60.02        8    53    zBCEFGHK
60.01        9    48    zBCEGHIJK
60.00        7    41    BCGHIJK
59.99        6    33    BCGHIJ
59.98        6    25    BCGHIJ
59.97        6    30    BCGHIJ
59.96        5    26    BCGIJ
59.95        2    19    BI
59.94        2    12    BI
59.93        2     4    BI
59.92        1     1    I

*CBOT Market Profile and Market Profile are registered trademarks of the
Chicago Board of Trade
Copyright Board of Trade of the City of Chicago 1984.  All Rights Reserved.

**11-24 Micro**: Opening sharply lower, the initial balance has a larger range than normal, most likely eliminating the possibility of a trend day or a large directional move early. Other timeframe sellers drive the market seven ticks lower in E and F periods. Other timeframe buyers launch an attack from there, initially forming a responsive buying extreme and taking the market much higher, almost to the levels of the previous day. Note that the activity of 11-23 and 11-24 is contained within the range of 11-20 where other timeframe participants seem to be in a big skirmish. The highs of 11-20, which are the prices which found good responsive selling, are this bull market's next reference point.

**11-24 Macro**: The range extensions show much more velocity to the upside. This imbalance is caused by aggressiveness on the part of the buyers, which, combined with the neutral day structure which closes strongly, indicates strength.

TRADING SIMULATOR - Based on the CBOT Market Profile*

DM 1287 13:20:00 59.86   O 59.49   H 59.86   L 59.30   V 1120  TB 89˚84   TV 731˚321
         11/24/87

```
59.86    0     0   X
59.85    1     2   K
59.84    1     7   K
59.83    1     8   K
59.82    2     4   JK
59.81    2     4   JK
59.80    2     4   JK
59.79    1     2   J
59.78    1     7   J
59.77    2     8   IJ
59.76    2     4   IJ
59.75    2     7   IJ
59.74    2    12   IJ
59.73    2    16   IJ
59.72    2    18   IJ
59.71    2    22   IJ
59.70    2    24   IJ
59.69    2    14   IJ
59.68    2    12   IJ
59.67    3     7   zIJ
59.66    3     8   zHI
59.65    3    13   zHI
59.64    3    12   zHI
59.63    5    24   zABHI
59.62    5    29   zABHI
59.61    5    38   zABHI
59.60    5    53   zABHI
59.59    4    51   zABH
59.58    4    50  - zABH
59.57    5    40   yzABH
59.56    5    27   yABGH
59.55    5    25   yABGH
59.54    6    22   yABDGH
59.53    7    26   yABCDGH
59.52    6    32   yBCDGH
59.51    6    42   yBCDGH
59.50    6    56   yBCDEG
59.49    6    68   OCDEGH
59.48    5    53   yCDEG
59.47    5    26   yCDEG
59.46    4    18   yCEG
59.45    4    17   yCEG
59.44    4    18   yCEG
59.43    4    13   yEFG
59.42    4    13   yEFG
59.41    4    17   yEFG
59.40    4    13   yEFG
59.39    4     9   yEFG
59.38    4    11   yEFG
59.37    4    22   yEFG
59.36    3    21   EFG
59.35    3    23   EFG
59.34    2    21   EF
59.33    2    13   EF
59.32    1     7   F
59.31    1     4   F
59.30    1     2   F
```

**11-25 Micro**: The market opens a bit higher and develops a large initial balance. The first sign of other timeframe activity comes in C period, where sellers move the market down three ticks below the initial balance. Other timeframe buyers come in at this point and rotate the market up and over the initial balance in D and E periods. Note that while both buying and selling range extensions fail to provide follow-through, buying shows a bit more velocity. The market moves into a two-timeframe auction the rest of the day. Again, the battle between the other timeframe seller and buyer is still being contested.

**11-25 Macro**: We see a tendency (in the last two days) for the other timeframe seller to come in early to extend the range below the initial balance by a few ticks, only to be followed by the other timeframe buyer, who moves the market much higher. In fact, both 11-24 and 11-25 see strong initiating activity on the buy side. We continue to look to the highs of the previous week, at 6038, and expect to see them at least tested due to the continuation of higher values.

TRADING SIMULATOR - Based on the CBOT Market Profile*

DM 1287 13:20:00 59.93  O 59.96  H 60.20  L 59.89  V  840 TB 76°56  TV 582°197
         11/25/87

| | | | |
|---|---|---|---|
| 60.20 | 0 | 0 | |
| 60.19 | 1 | 3 | E |
| 60.18 | 1 | 4 | E |
| 60.17 | 1 | 5 | E |
| 60.16 | 1 | 5 | E |
| 60.15 | 1 | 6 | E |
| 60.14 | 2 | 5 | DE |
| 60.13 | 2 | 8 | DE |
| 60.12 | 3 | 17 | zDE |
| 60.11 | 4 | 21 | yzDE |
| 60.10 | 5 | 31 | yzDEF |
| 60.09 | 5 | 36 | yzDEF |
| 60.08 | 5 | 33 | yzDEF |
| 60.07 | 6 | 27 | yzBDEF |
| 60.06 | 7 | 28 | yzBDEFG |
| 60.05 | 7 | 39 | yzBDEFG |
| 60.04 | 8 | 36 - | yzBDEFGH |
| 60.03 | 8 | 31 | yzBDEFGH |
| 60.02 | 6 | 34 | yzABGH |
| 60.01 | 8 | 48 | yzABDGHI |
| 60.00 | 9 | 59 | yzABCDGHI |
| 59.99 | 9 | 47 | yzABCDGHI |
| 59.98 | 8 | 58 | yzACDGHI |
| 59.97 | 8 | 61 | yzACGHIJ |
| 59.96 | 9 | 45 | OzACGHIJK |
| 59.95 | 7 | 42 | yACGIJK |
| 59.94 | 6 | 41 | yACIJK |
| 59.93 | 6 | 37 | yACIJX |
| 59.92 | 3 | 21 | yCJ |
| 59.91 | 1 | 7 | C |
| 59.90 | 1 | 3 | C |
| 59.89 | 1 | 1 | C |

**11-27 Micro**: A holiday market, this day is marked by a higher opening (above 6038) and an extremely quiet initial balance. As seen in the last few days, other timeframe sellers move the market below the initial balance, and then the other timeframe buyers come in the market and propel it upward. This end of the week session is also above the range of 11-20 and is marked by (what for a holiday market must be considered relatively strong) initiating buying which settles near the day's highs. Nervous shorts are covering while longs are displaying confidence, either staying long or adding on.

**11-27 Macro**: Opening above our reference point, the market breaks down early to test the support at the old highs. We attribute the lack of trade facilitation to holiday markets. The range extension move to the upside, plus the fact that the market closed well on the day and the week, bodes well for continuation. Note that again, for yet another week, prices move higher over time.

TRADING SIMULATOR - Based on the CBOT Market Profile*

DM 1287 13:19:35 60.64  O 60.47  H 60.70  L 60.37  V  587 TB 82^24  TV 380^169
11/27/87

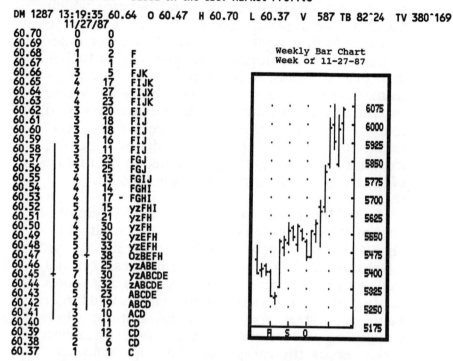

| 60.70 | 0 | 0 |  |
|---|---|---|---|
| 60.69 | 0 | 0 |  |
| 60.68 | 1 | 2 | F |
| 60.67 | 1 | 1 | F |
| 60.66 | 3 | 5 | FJK |
| 60.65 | 4 | 17 | FIJK |
| 60.64 | 4 | 27 | FIJX |
| 60.63 | 4 | 23 | FIJK |
| 60.62 | 3 | 20 | FIJ |
| 60.61 | 3 | 18 | FIJ |
| 60.60 | 3 | 18 | FIJ |
| 60.59 | 3 | 16 | FIJ |
| 60.58 | 3 | 11 | FIJ |
| 60.57 | 3 | 23 | FGJ |
| 60.56 | 3 | 25 | FGJ |
| 60.55 | 4 | 13 | FGIJ |
| 60.54 | 4 | 14 | FGHI |
| 60.53 | 4 | 17 - | FGHI |
| 60.52 | 5 | 15 | yzFHI |
| 60.51 | 4 | 21 | yzFH |
| 60.50 | 4 | 30 | yzFH |
| 60.49 | 5 | 30 | yzEFH |
| 60.48 | 5 | 33 | yzEFH |
| 60.47 | 6 | 38 | OzBEFH |
| 60.46 | 5 | 25 | yzABE |
| 60.45 | 7 | 30 | yzABCDE |
| 60.44 | 6 | 32 | zABCDE |
| 60.43 | 5 | 23 | ABCDE |
| 60.42 | 4 | 19 | ABCD |
| 60.41 | 3 | 10 | ACD |
| 60.40 | 2 | 11 | CD |
| 60.39 | 2 | 12 | CD |
| 60.38 | 2 | 6 | CD |
| 60.37 | 1 | 1 | C |

Weekly Bar Chart
Week of 11-27-87

*CBOT Market Profile and Market Profile are registered trademarks of the
Chicago Board of Trade
Copyright Board of Trade of the City of Chicago 1984.  All Rights Reserved.

**11-30 Micro**: The market opens 50 points higher and establishes an initial balance which indicates some profit-taking by longs. The single tick failure in A period is followed by other time-frame buyers probing, moving the market higher in D period, where they are met with other time-frame sellers who rapidly move the market lower, extending price below the initial balance by a good margin. The other timeframe buyers then counteract this move, creating a defined buying extreme. The trade is then contained in the middle of the range for the duration of the session.

**11-30 Macro**: An imbalanced profile, reminiscent of 10-20, the market's bounce occurring in F shows interested other timeframe buying, always a welcome sign for continued bullishness, but not sufficient to sustain such a move. This day shows the bullish information of higher values in a larger value area, but also shows bearishness when comparing the velocity of the range extension down versus the range extension up. Again, the bulls who stayed long through the weekend are rewarded and should consider taking profits. The big move made early in the week is difficult to sustain and is usually followed by some pull-back.

TRADING SIMULATOR - Based on the CBOT Market Profile*

DM 1287 13:20:29 61.23  O 61.25  H 61.35  L 60.98  V  944 TB 90^56  TV 272^593
         11/30/87
61.35      0      0
61.34      1      4    D
61.33      2      8    DE
61.32      2     14    DE
61.31      2     16    DE
61.30      3     15    yDE
61.29      5     18    yzCDE
61.28      5     28    yzCDE
61.27      5     36    yzCDE
61.26      6     38    yzBCDE
61.25      8     39    OzABCDEH
61.24      9     54    yzABCDEHJ
61.23     10     79    yzABCDEHJX
61.22     11     76    yzABCDEGHJK
61.21     11     56    yzABCDEGHJK
61.20     11     66    yzABCEGHIJK
61.19     11     72    yzABCEGHIJK
61.18     10     56    zABCEGHIJK
61.17      9     51    zABEFGHIJ
61.16      9     39  - zABEFGHIJ
61.15      7     23    AEFGHIJ
61.14      4     18    FGIJ
61.13      3     15    FIJ
61.12      3     16    FIJ
61.11      3     22    FIJ
61.10      3     18    FIJ
61.09      3      8    FIJ
61.08      2      7    FI
61.07      1      7    F
61.06      1      6    F
61.05      1      6    F
61.04      1      6    F
61.03      1      5    F
61.02      1      5    F
61.01      1      7    F
61.00      1      4    F
60.99      1      3    F
60.98      1      1    F

**12-01 Micro**: The day begins a bit lower, and the initial balance rallies upward. The other time-frame buyers move in during D period in thin December trade, extending beyond the initial balance. Price moves far enough, fast enough so that other timeframe sellers enter, leaving a small selling extreme and rotating the market past the other side of the initial balance. The market breaks late —not a welcome sign for the bulls.

**12-01: Macro**: The market rallies to a natural stopping place, and closes in the low end of the range, a sign of weakness. Another sign comes from the fact that the initial move up by the other timeframe buyers is neutralized by sellers later in the day. Buying imbalance may have ebbed for the time being. As we saw before, this late session type of activity coming from a neutral day structure may portend a continuation move in that direction (as we saw on 11-24 and 11-27). Interestingly, the market was contained by the price of 6150.

TRADING SIMULATOR - Based on the CBOT Market Profile*

```
DM 0388 13:20:04 61.13  O 61.13  H 61.50  L 61.07  V  297 TB 62`66  TV 184`91
         12/01/87
61.50    0    0
61.49    1    1    D
61.48    1    4    D
61.47    1    5    D
61.46    2    3    DE
61.45    3    7    DEF
61.44    2    7    DE
61.43    1    4    E
61.42    2    3    EF
61.41    3    4    DEF
61.40    2    4    EF
61.39    1    2    F
61.38    3    4    DEF
61.37    3    6    DFG
61.36    2    4    DF
61.35    3    5    DFG
61.34    2    2    zG
61.33    2    4    zG
61.32    2    3    zG
61.31    1    5    z
61.30    4    8    zCDGi
61.29    4    7    zCDG
61.28    4    7  - zCDG
61.27    5    8    yzACH
61.26    5   10    zABCD
61.25    6   12    yACDHJ
61.24    7   17    yABCDHJ
61.23    7   10    yABCDHJ
61.22    7   13    yABCDHJ
61.21    5   14    yABHJ
61.20    6   22    yABDHJ
61.19    6   17    yABHIJ
61.18    7   19    yABHIJK
61.17    6   13    yABHIJ
61.16    6   13    yAHIJK
61.15    5   11    AHIJK
61.14    3    5    yIK
61.13    4    4    OAHX
61.12    1    1    I
61.11    1    2    I
61.10    2    5    HI
61.09    0    0
61.08    0    0
61.07    1    1    I
```

*CBOT Market Profile and Market Profile are registered trademarks of the Chicago Board of Trade
Copyright Board of Trade of the City of Chicago 1984.  All Rights Reserved.

**12-02 Micro**: The opening sees price at the high
end of the previous day's value. It is also marked
by a small-to-normal sized initial balance. Other
timeframe buyers rally the market in D period,
but for the second day in a row, buyers do not
dominate the day's activity. The remainder of the
day only gets within three ticks of this high (in E
period), thus forming a selling extreme. Other
timeframe sellers again rotate the market back
down. The day closes in the bottom third of its
range in what might be termed sloppy price action
in a thin market.

**12-02 Macro**: With a lower low, a lower high,
and the fact that two timeframe activity has
become common in the last few days, another correction can be expected.

TRADING SIMULATOR - Based on the CBOT Market Profile*

DM 0388  13:19:42  61.12   O 61.27   H 61.37   L 61.04   V   267  TB 56^53   TV 111^137
         12/02/87

```
61.37    0     0
61.36    1     3    D
61.35    1     2    D
61.34    1     4    D
61.33    2     3    DE
61.32    1     2    D
61.31    0     0
61.30    2     2    DE
61.29    1     2    E
61.28    3     4    yDE
61.27    4    11    OBDE
61.26    2     8    BD
61.25    4    15    yBDE
61.24    3    13    yBD
61.23    8    18    yzABCDEF
61.22    6     8    yzABCD
61.21    7    13    yzABCDF
61.20    7    19  - yzABCEF
61.19    6    10    zABCEF
61.18    8    15    zABCFGHI
61.17    5    10    zACEI
61.16    6     8    zABCEG
61.15    5     8    zACEI
61.14    3     7    zGI
61.13    3     8    GHI
61.12    5     7    GHIJX
61.11    3    12    GHJ
61.10    5    14    GHIJK
61.09    5    12    GHIJK
61.08    3     7    GJK
61.07    4     8    GIJK
61.06    2     5    JK
61.05    2     4    JK
61.04    2     2    IJ
```

**12-03 Micro**: The day opens higher but quickly moves lower in thin but aggressive selling displaying aggressiveness. The other timeframe seller is responding to price above and then in value, as has been the case for several days. The market falls away, forming a large, early entry type of selling extreme, indicating that the high should be in for the day. The trade is then confined to the lower 1/3 to 1/2 of this initial balance.

**12-03 Macro**: The higher opening received responsive, aggressive selling that took the market below the previous session low, below the 6100 level (note the disparity of trades taking place at that price versus the comparatively small amount of time during which the price traded), to new lows on the week, and down to the high of 11-27. The pronounced imbalance with greater trade facilitation at lower values indicates that the correction is not over. Support can be expected at the lows of the previous week, at 5930.

TRADING SIMULATOR - Based on the CBOT Market Profile*

DM 0388 13:20:49 60.81   O 61.36   H 61.42   L 60.70   V   378  TB 80^81   TV 175^174
12/03/87

```
61.42    0    0
61.40    2    5   y
61.38    2    9   y
61.36    2    9   0
61.34    2   11   y
61.32    3    6   yz
61.30    2    3   y
61.28    2    3   yz
61.26    1    1   y
61.24    2    3   yz
61.22    1    1   y
61.20    2    3   yz
61.18    1    1   z
61.16    2    2   z
61.14    0    0
61.12    0    0
61.10    1    2   z
61.08    0    0
61.06    2    2  - z
61.04    1    2   z
61.02    3    7   zB
61.00    5   16   zAB
60.98    7   13   zABFH
60.96    7   11   zABFH
60.94   10   24   zABCFG
60.92   13   24   zABCDFGHI
60.90   16 + 42   zABCDEFGHI
60.88   18   37   zABCDEFGHI
60.86   14   24   zABCDEFGHI
60.84   15   26   zABCDEFGIK
60.82    9   13   zAIJK
60.80   12   24   zADEIJX
60.78    9   14   zAEIJK
60.76    4   14   zAJ
60.74    5   15   zAJ
60.72    3    5   AJ
60.70    2    2   zJ
```

*CBOT Market Profile and Market Profile are registered trademarks of the
Chicago Board of Trade
Copyright Board of Trade of the City of Chicago 1984.  All Rights Reserved.

**12-04 Micro**: The open is higher with a much smaller initial balance than the previous session. A period breaks through the initial balance to the down side, which is the expected continuation of recent responsive selling activity. The other time-frame seller controls the market until H period, which moves down in a one timeframe manner. Only in the last three time periods is any buying activity present. The buying extreme is minimal and the market settles in the bottom third of the day.

**12-04 Macro**: The higher opening was a price above value in a market that had recently seen aggressive responsive and initiating selling. The A period single print selling range extension was the first such high velocity move since the buying range extension on 11-18, which was much stronger. Unable to continue at this level of activity, this day may be some sort of selling climax. On the other hand, the fact that the market made new lows on the week, particularly on Friday, does not indicate tremendous strength to the fainthearted bull. Only the bull market climax paradox (see macro analysis, 11-20), plus the fact that the market didn't close on the low of the day (and week) indicates some tentativeness on the part of bears to remain confidently short. While price didn't move higher over time, the market remains comfortably above the previous week's lows. For the following week, this day's lows will provide some semblance of support.

TRADING SIMULATOR - Based on the CBOT Market Profile*

DM 0388 13:20:03 60.57  O 61.10  H 61.15  L 60.31  V  450 TB 118^71 TV 173^264
         12/04/87

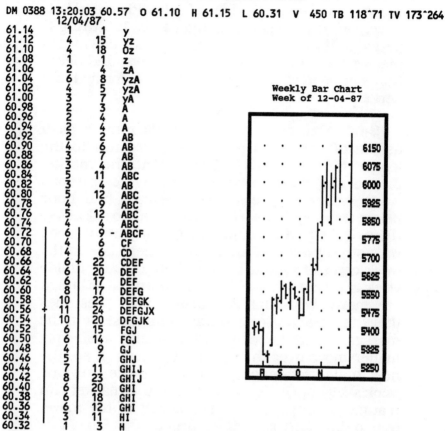

```
61.14     1      1    y
61.12     4     15    yz
61.10     4     18    Oz
61.08     1      1    z
61.06     2      4    zA
61.04     6      8    yzA
61.02     4      5    yzA
61.00     3      7    yA
60.98     2      3    A
60.96     2      4    A
60.94     2      4    A
60.92     2      2    AB
60.90     4      6    AB
60.88     3      7    AB
60.86     3      4    AB
60.84     5     11    ABC
60.82     3      4    AB
60.80     5     12    ABC
60.78     4      9    ABC
60.76     5     12    ABC
60.74     4      4    ABC
60.72     6      9  - ABCF
60.70     4      6    CF
60.68     4      6    CD
60.66     6  +  22    CDEF
60.64     6     20    DEF
60.62     6     17    DEF
60.60     8     17    DEFG
60.58    10     22    DEFGK
60.56    11     24    DEFGJX
60.54    10     20    DFGJK
60.52     6     15    FGJ
60.50     6     14    FGJ
60.48     4      9    GJ
60.46     5      7    GHJ
60.44     7     11    GHIJ
60.42     8     23    GHIJ
60.40     6     20    GHI
60.38     6     18    GHI
60.36     6     12    GHI
60.34     3     11    HI
60.32     1      3    H
```

Weekly Bar Chart
Week of 12-04-87

6150
6075
6000
5925
5850
5775
5700
5625
5550
5475
5400
5325
5250

A  S  O  N

**12-07 Micro**: Opening near the previous week's settlement, the market has a fairly wide initial balance. Other timeframe selling comes in during C period and the rest of the day follows a downward bias with the day closing near its lows, and below that week's lows. A buying extreme is formed in J period.

**12-07 Macro**: The only significantly bullish aspect of this day's activity as it relates to the longer term involves the fact that the market dipped slightly below the lows of the previous week —spending less than a single half hour below this key support — and then closed above them. If the pattern of weakness early in the week with strength and a strong settlement late in the week comes to pass, the possibility of an outside week is raised, a very bullish structure this late in the move. With this scenario, which presumes that the previous session was a climax sell-off, the market would be expected to bring a sharply higher move over the coming sessions. If so, the next major reference point will be the previous week's highs, 6149. Above them, the market can resume perhaps the fastest ascent of the move, due to the maturity of the market.

TRADING SIMULATOR - Based on the CBOT Market Profile*

DM 0388 13:20:17 60.37  O 60.60  H 60.70  L 60.28  V  663 TB 50^81  TV 227^393
        12/07/87

```
60.70    0     0
60.69    2     3   yz
60.68    2     3   yz
60.67    2     6   yz
60.66    2     8   yz
60.65    2    13   yz
60.64    3    16   yzB
60.63    3     7   yzB
60.62    3    14   yzB
60.61    4    24   yzAB
60.60    5    25   OzABE
60.59    5    20   yzABE
60.58    5    26   yABDE
60.57    6    29   yABDEF
60.56    6    32   yABCDE
60.55  ← 7 ↓  43   yABCDEF
60.54    6    42   yACDEF
60.53    6    26   yACDEF
60.52    5    15   yCDEF
60.51    5    14   yCDEF
60.50    4    21   CDFG
60.49    4    20 - CDFG
60.48    4    14   CDFG
60.47    4    13   CFGH
60.46    3    17   FGH
60.45    3    15   FGH
60.44    3    13   FGH
60.43    3    15   FGH
60.42    2    10   GH
60.41    3     7   GHI
60.40    3     9   GHI
60.39    2    10   HI
60.38    2    14   HI
60.37    3    17   HIX
60.36    4    14   HIJK
60.35    3    12   IJK
60.34    3     8   IJK
60.33    2     6   JK
60.32    2    13   JK
60.31    2    17   JK
60.30    1    18   J
60.29    1    12   J
60.28    1     1   J
```

**12-08 Micro:** This day opens higher, trading where value has been developed during the previous session. The other timeframe activity is initially down but not vociferously so, and is soon rejected by a single print in D period. The majority of transactions occur around the initial balance. H period follows E period's move up through the opening price. Trade stays above or near the opening price for the remainder of the session and closes well.

**12-08 Macro:** While not a broad facilitation of trade day, the market did build higher values. The quietness in the market is occurring due to a trade balance report to be released two days hence. Because of this, the fact that the market is higher but quieter is discounted somewhat.

TRADING SIMULATOR - Based on the CBOT Market Profile*

```
DM 0388 13:19:58 60.80  O 60.68  H 60.82  L 60.56  V  561  TB 58^41  TV 317^177
         12/08/87
60.82        0     0
60.81        2     7    HI
60.80        3    17    HIX
60.79        3    14    HIK
60.78        3     7    HIK
60.77        4     7    HIJK
60.76        3    12    HIJ
60.75        3    20    HIJ
60.74        3    20    HIJ
60.73   |    3    21    HIJ
60.72   |    3    20    HIJ
60.71   |    3    18    HIJ
60.70   |    3    21    EHJ
60.69   |    3    20  - EHJ
60.68   |    4    16    OEHJ
60.67   |    6    19    yADEGH
60.66   |    7    29    yABDEGH
60.65  -+-  10  |  46    yzABCDEFGH
60.64   |    9  -+  67    yzABCDEFG
60.63   |    8    66    yzABCDFG
60.62   |    8    40    yzABCDFG
60.61   |    6    21    zABCDF
60.60   |    4    20    zBCD
60.59   |    2    13    CD
60.58   |    2     8    CD
60.57   |    2     6    CD
60.56        1     3    D
```

**12-09 Micro**: Another higher opening is wit-
nessed, again with a very small initial balance.
The market probes downward in B period as the
other timeframe sellers become active. Scoring
lower drives, the sellers hold control until F
period, where a buying extreme is formed. Finally,
other timeframe buyers push the market back up
to the initial balance, before settling it in the middle of the day's range. Overall, this day has a very
small range and is quiet.

**12-09 Macro**: An even quieter day, albeit with
higher values. Market-generated information
indicates some bullishness from the fact that participants are "evening up" prior to the report —
usual behavior in a market where both buyers
and sellers exit their positions, decreasing open
interest. A market experiencing quiet but higher
values directly prior to a report can be interpreted
as a sign of strength, because the market is
indicating that the "weak hands" are the shorts,
and that longs are confident, not caring to exit
prior to the report in great numbers — hence the
higher values. In other words, major reports are
often market-imposed catalysts for change, and
their existence often forces the less dominant
other timeframe group to exit. Given that movement in values suggests that shorts must be
covering in greater numbers than their counterparts, we remain bullish.

TRADING SIMULATOR - Based on the CBOT Market Profile*

DM 0388  13:20:14 60.86  O 60.94  H 60.96  L 60.75  V  563  TB 41ˇ41  TV 235ˇ265
          12/09/87
```
60.96        0      0
60.95        1      1    y
60.94        3     15    OzA
60.93        3     30    yzA
60.92        3     26    yzA
60.91        5     17    yzABH
60.90        6     22    yzBCDH
60.89        7     31    yzBCDGH
60.88        6     35    BCDGHK
60.87        8     57    BCDEGHJK
60.86        8     63    BCDEGHJX
60.85        7     55  - BCDEGHJ
60.84        8     46    BCDEGHIJ
60.83        5     27    EGHIJ
60.82        6     37    EFGHIJ
60.81        5     39    EFGIJ
60.80        4     19    EFIJ
60.79        3     10    EFI
60.78        1     14    F
60.77        2     12    EF
60.76        1      5    F
60.75        1      1    F
```

*CBOT Market Profile and Market Profile are registered trademarks of the
Chicago Board of Trade
Copyright Board of Trade of the City of Chicago 1984.  All Rights Reserved.

**12-10 Micro**: A point and a half initial balance
rally off of the balance of trade data marks the
day.       The     self-adjusting      through      overcompensation forms two large extremes on both
ends of the day's value. The day builds value
above the previous week's highs, around the middle of the very wide initial balance. The market
closes on the high end of the range, further evi-
dence of a strong market.

**12-10 Macro**: Having reacted favorably to the
report by forcing prices above the resistance of the
previous week's high (6149), the other timeframe
buyer is firmly in control of this market. Having
peeked below the previous week's low and now
rallied sharply in reaction to the report, an outside
week is now apparent, a very strong indicator —
perhaps that we're nearing the climax phase.

TRADING SIMULATOR - Based on the CBOT Market Profile*

DM 0388 13:20:10 61.92  O 60.81  H 62.30  L 60.65  V 1468 TB 96˜93  TV 880˜521
        12/10/87

```
62.28    0    0
62.25    0    0
62.22    0    0
62.19    1    1   y
62.16    0    0
62.13    0    0
62.10    1    3   y
62.07    0    0
62.04    1    1   y
62.01    0    0
61.98    1    2   y
61.95    2    4   y
61.92    4   13   JX
61.89    7   68   yJK
61.86    4   71   JK
61.83    8   32   yFIJ
61.80   14   57   yCFGIJ
61.77   18  112   BCFGHI
61.74   20  165   yBCFGHI
61.71   21  172   BCEFGHI
61.68   18  111   yzBCEFGH
61.65   16  134   yzBCDE
61.62   17  142   zABCDE
61.59   14  120   yzABD
61.56   12   47   yzABD
61.53    7   45   yzAD
61.50    5   41   yzA
61.47    3   29  - A
61.44    4   12   yA
61.41    3   12   A
61.38    3    4   yA
61.35    1    1   y
61.32    0    0
61.29    1    1   y
61.26    0    0
61.23    1    1   y
61.20    1    1   y
61.17    0    0
61.14    1    1   y
61.11    0    0
61.08    1    1   y
61.05    0    0
61.02    0    0
60.99    1    2   y
60.96    0    0
60.93    0    0
60.90    1    1   y
60.87    0    0
60.84    1    1   y
60.81    1    1   yO
60.78    3   12   y
60.75    3   24   y
60.72    3   12   y
60.69    3    6   y
60.66    1    2   y
```

**12-11 Micro**: Opening around the close of the previous session, a small initial balance is formed. Responsive other timeframe selling is evident in the beginning of the day, with a B period selling range extension. Other timeframe buyers come into the market in this same period, and create a buying extreme. The rest of the day moves gradually up in a two timeframe mode. More buying activity is observed with an E period range extension. This rest day settles in the upper third of the day's range.

**12-11 Macro**: The day builds value above the previous session's values, and develops without a defined selling extreme. The week settles toward the high end of this outside week's high-low range (6028-6220), signaling the continued bull move.

TRADING SIMULATOR - Based on the CBOT Market Profile*

DM 0388 13:20:16 62.01  O 61.99  H 62.08  L 61.81  V  802 TB 34ˆ80  TV 215ˆ520
         12/11/87

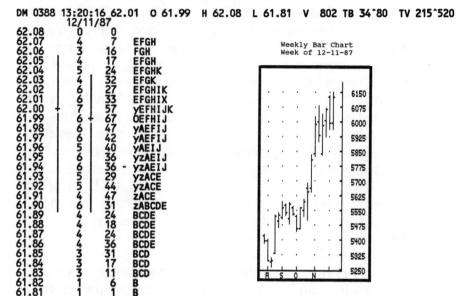

| 62.08 | 0 | 0  |        |
|-------|---|----|--------|
| 62.07 | 4 | 7  | EFGH   |
| 62.06 | 3 | 16 | FGH    |
| 62.05 | 4 | 17 | EFGH   |
| 62.04 | 5 | 24 | EFGHK  |
| 62.03 | 4 | 32 | EFGK   |
| 62.02 | 6 | 27 | EFGHIK |
| 62.01 | 6 | 33 | EFGHIX |
| 62.00 | 7 | 57 | yEFHIJK |
| 61.99 | 6 | 67 | OEFHIJ |
| 61.98 | 6 | 47 | yAEFIJ |
| 61.97 | 6 | 42 | yAEFIJ |
| 61.96 | 5 | 40 | yAEIJ  |
| 61.95 | 6 | 36 | yzAEIJ |
| 61.94 | 6 | 36 | yzAEIJ |
| 61.93 | 5 | 29 | yzACE  |
| 61.92 | 5 | 44 | yzACE  |
| 61.91 | 4 | 47 | zACE   |
| 61.90 | 6 | 31 | zABCDE |
| 61.89 | 4 | 24 | BCDE   |
| 61.88 | 4 | 18 | BCDE   |
| 61.87 | 4 | 24 | BCDE   |
| 61.86 | 4 | 36 | BCDE   |
| 61.85 | 3 | 31 | BCD    |
| 61.84 | 3 | 17 | BCD    |
| 61.83 | 3 | 11 | BCD    |
| 61.82 | 1 | 6  | B      |
| 61.81 | 1 | 1  | B      |

Weekly Bar Chart
Week of 12-11-87

**12-14 Micro**: Opening higher by over 25 ticks,
this day develops a small initial balance. C period
breaks both sides of the initial balance, first to the
upside and then to the downside, as other timeframe sellers become more dominant. C period
rallies past the opening reference point with
velocity, but curiously falls away, leaving a
defined selling extreme. D period goes down further still, with E period continuing this weak
activity. At these prices, other timeframe buyers
cannot resist coming in and moving the market
up. This buying activity forms a meager buying
extreme, and the rest of the day's activity stays in
the bottom third of this double distribution trend
day's range.

**12-14 Macro**: This day was a curious one for the
day trader. So solid a range extension as that
which occurred up in C period usually portends
for directional continuation. Clearly a day dominated by selling, this type of quiet, double distribution profile is usual in holiday markets. As
stated before, weak activity early in the week is
not as technically damaging as that same selling
activity late in the week, so we can presume the
bull market remains intact until profile activity
and a violation of last week's lows indicate otherwise. Again, this week can be expected to bring the
holiday market's low volatility and non-facilitating
behavior, brought on by a holiday-motivated
shortage of interested other timeframe
participants.

TRADING SIMULATOR - Based on the CBOT Market Profile*

DM 0388 13:19:58 62.06  O 62.28  H 62.33  L 61.95  V  776 TB 75ˆ44  TV 161ˆ556
        12/14/87

```
62.33   0 |  0
62.32   1 | 12   C
62.31   1 | 19   C
62.30   1 | 12   C
62.29   1 |  6   C
62.28   3 |  9   OAC
62.27   4 | 14   yzAC
62.26   5 | 31   yzABC
62.25   5 | 54   yzABC
62.24   6 ⊦ 59   yzABCD
62.23   6 | 41   yzABCD
62.22   5 | 33   yABCD
62.21   5 | 32   yABCD
62.20   4 | 20   ABCD
62.19   4 | 15   ABCD
62.18   2 | 12   CD
62.17   2 |  6   CD
62.16   2 |  5   CD
62.15   1 |  4   D
62.14   1 |  1 - D
62.13   1 |  2   D
62.12   1 |  3   D
62.11   1 |  2   D
62.10   1 |  1   D
62.09   3 |  3   DFG
62.08   6 | 25   DEFGJK
62.07   7 | 43   DEFGHJK
62.06   8 ⊦ 47   DEFGHIJX
62.05   7 | 43   DEFGHIJ
62.04   7 | 45   DEFGHIJ
62.03   7 | 47   DEFGHIJ
62.02   6 | 32   DEFHIJ
62.01   5 | 25   DEFHI
62.00   5 | 27   DEFHI
61.99   3 | 19   EFI
61.98   2 | 11   EI
61.97   2 |  6   EI
61.96   1 |  4   E
61.95   1 |  2   E
```

**12-15 Micro**: This day opens higher, and has a small initial balance which nevertheless indicates (by the opening remaining the high) that selling was evident in a non-aggressive manner from the opening bell — all clues indicate a selling trend day may be possible. After an A period test of the highs, other timeframe selling appears in C period as well as in D, F, and G periods. Below the lows of the previous session, buying is finally attracted in G period, forming a buying extreme. The market rallies over half way back of the day's range and closes in the bottom third.

**12-15 Macro**: Selling, as aggressive initiating activity, predominates this session. Because of the holiday market environment, we would not expect to see as wide-ranging and volatile a session as that which occurs during the height of business activity. Holiday markets tend not to display follow-through, and the average range of a market is relatively small.

**TRADING SIMULATOR - Based on the CBOT Market Profile\***

```
DM 0388 13:19:56 61.88  O 62.14  H 62.15  L 61.78  V  659 TB 84^38  TV 286^335
         12/15/87
62.15    0     0
62.14    2     7    OA
62.13    2    17    yA
62.12    3    28    yzA
62.11    4    38    yzAB
62.10    5    38    yzABC
62.09    4    24    zABC
62.08    3    19    zBC
62.07    3    13    zCE
62.06    2     6    CE
62.05    3    15    CEF
62.04    3    17    CEF
62.03    3     7    CEF
62.02    3    10    CEF
62.01    5    18    CDEFI
62.00    5    28    CDEFI
61.99    5    38    CDEFI
61.98    5    32    CDEFI
61.97    4    21    DEFI
61.96    5    19  - DEFGI
61.95    5    20    DFGIJ
61.94    5    19    DFGIJ
61.93    5    24    DFGIJ
61.92    6    23    DFGHIJ
61.91    5    18    FGHIJ
61.90    6    17    FGHIJK
61.89    4    17    GHJK
61.88    5    30    GHIJX
61.87    5    25    GHIJK
61.86    4    12    GHIJ
61.85    3     7    GHI
61.84    2     5    GH
61.83    2    12    GH
61.82    2    14    GH
61.81    1     7    G
61.80    1     7    G
61.79    1     5    G
61.78    1     1    G
```

\*CBOT Market Profile and Market Profile are registered trademarks of the
Chicago Board of Trade
Copyright Board of Trade of the City of Chicago 1984.  All Rights Reserved.

**12-16 Micro**: Opening above yesterday's close, this day has a normal to small initial balance. Other timeframe sellers issue the first attack as they drive the market below the initial balance in A and again in C periods. The low prices in C period coax the other timeframe buyers to accumulate, propping the market higher. This forms a defined buying extreme in C period at 6175. Other timeframe buyers continue their campaign upward to form buying range extensions in D, E, F, and J periods. The day closes two ticks from its highs.

**12-16 Macro**: The day again displays the responsive buyer creating a two-sided market. The market fails to fall below the previous session's lows, and then rallies late, nearing the highs of the session, a bullish sign. A neutral day structure with late activity and a defined close, this could be the start of continuation up, perhaps the final, climactic phase, if the outside week scenario is to hold. See comments made in macro analysis, 12-01.

```
TRADING SIMULATOR - Based on the CBOT Market Profile*

DM 0388 13:19:50 62.06  O 61.96  H 62.09  L 61.75  V  693 TB 48^57  TV 233^414
         12/16/87
62.09        0     0
62.08        1     7   J
62.07        2    19   JK
62.06        3    29   FJX
62.05        4    21   EFJK
62.04        3    13   EFJ
62.03        3     7   EFJ
62.02        4     9   EFHJ
62.01        4    20   EFHJ
62.00        6    30   DEFHIJ
61.99        6    35   DEFHIJ
61.98        6    41   DEFGHI
61.97        7  + 46   DEFGHIJ
61.96     +  8    40   ODEFGHIJ
61.95        6    28   yDEFGI
61.94        3    17   yDG
61.93        2    15   yG
61.92        3    19  - yDG
61.91        3    20   yzD
61.90        4    24   yzAD
61.89        3    27   zAD
61.88        3    23   zAD
61.87        3    20   zAD
61.86        3    18   zAD
61.85        2    12   AD
61.84        3     9   ABD
61.83        3    19   ABD
61.82        4    33   ABCD
61.81        4    32   ABCD
61.80        3    19   ABC
61.79        3    16   ABC
61.78        2    12   AC
61.77        1     7   C
61.76        1     3   C
61.75        1     1   C
```

**12-17 Micro**: This day opens higher and develops what a few weeks ago would be considered a very small, but now must be considered a normal sized, initial balance in the context of the holiday market conditions. Other timeframe activity comes into the market in D period as buyers push the market higher forming a buying range extension. The day then develops value in these higher regions with more buying in the form of range extensions in the G and K periods. The day closes on its high.

**12-17 Macro**: The market seems very strong, moving above the previous session's high in the initial balance, range extending to make new highs of the week — which are new highs on the move — and then closing at the highs of the day. While bulls would rather have seen more single print TPOs by the end of the day's trade (only three ticks between 6218-21), this is not necessarily an indication of weakness, since the holiday climate is the overriding factor. A previous pattern has established the low end of the previous day's higher distribution (or at worst the low of the single ticks) as significant support, which is tested on the next day. So long as the previous session's low end of the higher distribution holds as support during 12-18's session, this market should move significantly over the next several sessions. Is the holiday market condition influencing the market's behavior near settlement? It could very well be that short timeframe participants may be less interested in carrying inventory overnight in these thin conditions, where presumably a news or fundamental announcement may be grossly overreacted to due to the absence of the buffering other timeframe participants.

TRADING SIMULATOR - Based on the CBOT Market Profile*

DM 0388 13:19:54 62.37  O 62.14  H 62.37  L 62.04  V  728 TB 35^83  TV 215^461
          12/17/87
```
62.37      0      0   X
62.36      1      1   K
62.35      2      4   GK
62.34      3     14   GJK
62.33      4     27   GIJK
62.32      6     27   EGHIJK
62.31      6     24   EGHIJK
62.30      7     32   DEFGHIJ
62.29      7     36   DEFGHIJ
62.28  ┼   7     49   DEFGHIJ
62.27      6  ┼  52   DEFGHJ
62.26      6     51   DEFGHJ
62.25      6     41   DEFGHJ
62.24      5     24   DEFHJ
62.23      3     14   DEF
62.22      2      8   DE
62.21      1      3   D
62.20      1      1 - D
62.19      1      4   D
62.18      2      6   yD
62.17      2      8   yD
62.16      3     27   yCD
62.15      4     33   yzCD
62.14      5     23   OzACD
62.13      5     25   yzACD
62.12      5     33   yzABC
62.11      5     33   yzABC
62.10      5     35   yzABC
62.09      4     29   zABC
62.08      3     15   zAC
62.07      3     15   zAC
62.06      2     18   zC
62.05      2     12   zC
62.04      2      3   zC
```

*CBOT Market Profile and Market Profile are registered trademarks of the
Chicago Board of Trade
Copyright Board of Trade of the City of Chicago 1984.  All Rights Reserved.

**12-18 Micro**: This day opens below the single TPOs of 12-17, signaling a potential problem for the bulls. The opening hour displays a normal to large sized holiday market initial balance. Other timeframe selling enters the market early, confirming the problem for bulls, and A period extends downward. This selling activity continues for the remainder of the day with only a slight bounce up in I, J, and K periods. The market closes in the lower one-fifth of the day's range.

**12-18 Macro**: There should be no joy in Mudville for the bulls. The market on this day, particularly given the fact that it is the end of a week, indicates that the bull move either has made or is very near to making a climax, and for all but the most devout bulls, profits should be taken on the next rally. The fact that a strong trend day down that scores new lows on the week (and nearly closes on those lows) follows strong initiating buying is cause for major concern. Clearly, though, this week to week volatility is not unprecedented. In fact, as noted earlier, this ebb and flow behavior on a weekly basis is characteristic of a market near a major top. Note that between the weeks beginning 11-02 through this one, strong closes on the week have alternated with weak closes for the next week. Nevertheless, the only sign of continuation is a pattern similar to that seen during the week of 12-07: a lower low followed by a higher high and a strong settlement during the following week.

TRADING SIMULATOR - Based on the CBOT Market Profile*

DM 0388 13:19:58 61.72  O 62.15  H 62.18  L 61.61  V  966 TB 117ˆ49 TV 349ˆ577
12/18/87

```
62.18    0     0
62.17    1     5    y
62.16    1     6    y
62.15    1    16    O
62.14    2    17    yz
62.13    2     9    yz
62.12    2     8    yz
62.11    2     9    yz
62.10    2     6    yz
62.09    3    12    yzA
62.08    3    29    yzA
62.07    3    36    yzA
62.06    2    25    zA
62.05    2    11    zA
62.04    2     2    zA
62.03    1     3    A
62.02    2     4    AB
62.01    2     7    AB
62.00    3    13    ABD
61.99    4    16    ABCD
61.98    4    21    ABCD
61.97    4    24    ABCD
61.96    4    27    ABCD
61.95    4    38    ABCD
61.94    4    40    ABCD
61.93    4    34    ABCD
61.92    4    32    ABCD
61.91    3    23    ACD
61.90    4    17    ACDF
61.89    3    13  - ADF
61.88    3     9    ADF
61.87    3     9    ADF
61.86    3    12    ADF
61.85    4    16    ADEF
61.84    3    17    DEF
61.83    3    13    DEF
61.82    3    10    DEF
61.81    4    14    DEFG
61.80    3    14    EFG
61.79    3    19    EFG
61.78    5    25    EFGHJ
61.77    5    28    EFGHJ
61.76    6    34    EFGHJK
61.75    5    31    EGHJK
61.74    5    34    EGHJK
61.73    5    32    EGHJK
61.72    5    23    EGHJX
61.71    4    16    EHIJ
61.70    4    11    EHIJ
61.69    3     6    EHI
61.68    3     7    EHI
61.67    3    12    EHI
61.66    3    14    EHI
61.65    3    10    EHI
61.64    2    15    HI
61.63    2    18    HI
61.62    2     8    HI
61.61    1     1    H
```

Weekly Bar Chart
Week of 12-18-87

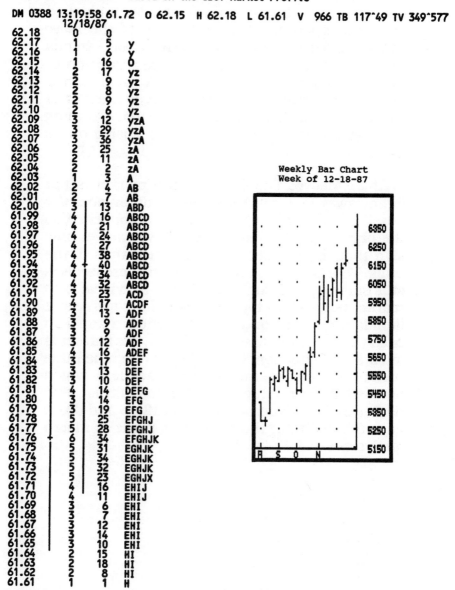

**12-21 Micro**: Opening higher by 16 ticks, this day has a small initial balance. The day is plagued with indecision early, as is typical of the more thinly traded holiday markets. A period extends the range meagerly to the downside with B probing the opposite side, and so on. A small buying extreme is formed in D period. The remainder of the day goes up in a one timeframe mode forming a range extension in J period and closing on its high.

**12-21 Macro**: The fact that the market is not falling away in a trend day fashion diminishes the possibility that the market may have topped. Also the presence of two-sided volatility is a welcome sign that the market is still in the hands of the bulls. This is because the market at these levels is still showing the tug-of-war that is typical of a market putting in a top, as opposed to the massive liquidating behavior exhibited when a top has been put in. In the case of the latter, the market is often a one directional, liquidating one timeframe break (not unlike the previous session) which occurs for several days in a row. In contrast, this day's structure resembles that of 12-16 and those days alluded to in the comments made in macro analysis, 12-01.

TRADING SIMULATOR - Based on the CBOT Market Profile*

DM 0388 13:20:12 61.99  O 61.88  H 62.00  L 61.71  V  464 TB 51^39  TV 197^228
         12/21/87

```
62.00    0     0
61.99    2    12   JX
61.98    2     3   JK
61.97    1     3   J
61.96    1     8   J
61.95    1     9   J
61.94    1     4   J
61.93    2     6   BJ
61.92    2    12   BJ
61.91    2    16   BJ
61.90    2    11   BJ
61.89    4     5   yBIJ
61.88    4    12   OBIJ
61.87    3    17   yBI
61.86    4    22   yABI
61.85    6    22 - yzABCI
61.84    6    26   yzACGI
61.83    6    39   yzACGH
61.82    7    39   yzACGHI
61.81    7    37   yzACDGH
61.80    7    31   yzACDGH
61.79    4    19   ACDG
61.78    5    15   ACDEG
61.77    5    17   CDEFG
61.76    3    16   DEF
61.75    3    19   DEF
61.74    3    18   DEF
61.73    2     9   DE
61.72    1     6   D
61.71    1     2   D
```

**12-22 Micro**: The open is lower and has a normal to small initial balance. Other timeframe buying comes into the market in C period. This continues in D, F, H, and J periods. Value develops in these higher areas.

**12-22 Macro:** Again, a two timeframe rotational market combined with a higher high is constructive, because a liquidation top is the only alternative. The buying imbalance is welcome, although the low of the previous week has not been pierced and rejected, as is needed to neutralize such a poor showing as that of 12-18.

TRADING SIMULATOR - Based on the CBOT Market Profile*

DM 0388 13:19:57 61.97  O 61.88  H 62.06  L 61.82  V  433 TB 30ˆ46  TV 154ˆ239
         12/22/87
62.06      0      0
62.05      1      3    J
62.04      3     19    HIJ
62.03      3     27    HIJ
62.02      5     21    FGHIJ
62.01      5     21    FGHIJ
62.00      6     25    DFGHIJ
61.99      8     36    DEFGHIJK
61.98  ÷   8  ÷  40    DEFGHIJK
61.97      5     26    DEFGX
61.96      3     15    DEF
61.95      4     18    CDEF
61.94      3     17  - CDE
61.93      2      9    CE
61.92      2      8    CE
61.91      2      6    yC
61.90      2      8    yC
61.89      2      8    yC
61.88      2     18    OC
61.87      2     15    yC
61.86      5     16    yzABC
61.85      5     25    yzABC
61.84      4     24    zABC
61.83      3     19    zAB
61.82      1      7    z

*CBOT Market Profile and Market Profile are registered trademarks of the
Chicago Board of Trade
Copyright Board of Trade of the City of Chicago 1984.  All Rights Reserved.

**12-23 Micro**: The open is low enough to pierce the low of the previous week. The initial balance develops a larger than normal holiday market range, and the other timeframe buying activity carries on, creating a range extension that continues through H period. The market moves back away from these highs and closes on the lower end of the upper third of the day's range.

**12-23 Macro**: Note that the low of the day, in piercing the support at the previous week's low, finds a buying extreme. This is also the second day in a row where responsive buying has created a significant buying range extension. If we do not see selling, then the outside week scenario could be seen again.

TRADING SIMULATOR - Based on the CBOT Market Profile*

DM 0388 13:19:59 61.66  O 61.62  H 61.75  L 61.46  V  676 TB 69^64  TV 280^347
         12/23/87

```
61.75    0     0
61.74    1     1   H
61.73    3     9   HIJ
61.72    4    19   HIJK
61.71    4    17   HIJK
61.70    5    16   FHIJK
61.69    4     9   HIJK
61.68    5    12   FHIJK
61.67    5    22   FHIJK
61.66    5    22   FHIJX
61.65    6    23   CFHIJK
.61.64   7    25   CFGHIJK
61.63    8    29   yCFGHIJK
61.62    7    34   OCEFGIJ
61.61    6    41   yCEGHI
61.60    8    49  - yCDEFGHI
61.59    8    31   yCDEFGHI
61.58    7    27   yACDEFG
61.57    6    32   yABCDE
61.56    7    36   yzABCDE
61.55    7    35   yzABCDE
61.54    7    24   yzABCDE
61.53    5    32   zABDE
61.52    5    40   zABDE
61.51    5    32   zABDE
61.50    4    15   zADE
61.49    3    11   zAD
61.48    1    16   z
61.47    1    12   z
61.46    1     4   z
```

**12-24 Micro**: Opening 20 points higher, the market advertises for other timeframe selling but receives none. Z period moves higher, leaving an initiating buying extreme which is tested in C and again in D period. The buyers find confidence with the market and proceed to rally it in a dramatic one timeframe move. The market settles near the highs on this pre-holiday abbreviated session.

**12-24 Macro**: The strong buying that was found in this session is significant, bringing the market to levels above the previous week's high, 6237. The bull market resumes with this turnaround week.

```
DM 0387
12/24/87

6250  HI
6249  HI
6248  HI
6247  HI
6246  HIJ
6245  GH
6244  GH
6243  GH
6242  GH
6241  GH
6240  GH
6239  GH
6238  GH
6237  GH
6236  GH
6235  GH
6234  GH
6233  GH
6232  G
6231  G
6230  G
6229  G
6228  G
6227  G
6226  G
6225  G
6224  G
6223  G
6222  G
6221  G
6220  G
6219  G
6218  G
6217  G
6216  G
6215  G
6214  G
6213  FG
6212  FG
6211  EFG
6210  EFG
6209  EFG
6208  EFG
6207  EFG
6206  EFG
6205  EG
6204  EG
6203  EG
6202  EG
6201  E
6200  E
6199  zE
6198  zADE
6197  zACDE
6196  zABCDE
6195  zABCD
6194  yzABCD
6193  yzABCD
6192  yzABCD
6191  yCD
6190  yD
6189  y
6188  y
6187  y
```

(C) 1984 CBOT

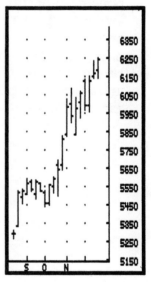

Weekly Bar Chart
Week of 12-25-87

**12-28 Micro**: An early entry buying extreme —
from an opening almost 50 points higher than the
settlement of 12-24 — starts the day. Sharply
higher prices advertise for other timeframe selling, but the market receives no selling response.
The initial balance is wide and made up entirely of
Y period. A period extends the initial balance on
the buy side. This market facilitates trade the rest
of the day; although it closes very poorly for a
strong bull market.

**12-28 Macro**: Note the intra-day back and forth
movement of this market. This is frenzied activity,
particularly when taken in the context of the holiday market conditions. Given the age of this bull
move, and the recent directional move followed by
the zig zag type of activity seen on almost a weekly
basis between buyers and sellers, clearly a crescendo must be near.

TRADING SIMULATOR - Based on the CBOT Market Profile*

DM 0388 13:19:49 63.07  O 63.02  H 63.41  L 63.02  V  932 TB 72ˆ104 TV 433ˆ436
          12/28/87

```
63.41    0      0
63.40    2     12    HI
63.39    3     16    AHI
63.38    3     12    AHI
63.37    3     14    AHI
63.36    4     24    ADHI
63.35    4     25    ADHI
63.34    6 |   21    ADEGHI
63.33    6 |   23    ADEGHI
63.32    7 |   26    ADEGHIJ
63.31    7 |   25    ADEGHIJ
63.30    8 |   35    yABDEGHJ
63.29    8 |   41    yABDEGHJ
63.28    9 |   47    yABCDEGHJ
63.27  ╪ 9 |   51    yzABCDEGJ
63.26    8 |   59    yABCDEGJ
63.25    8 ╪  63    yzABCEGJ
63.24    8 |   49    yzABCEGJ
63.23    7 |   36    yzABEGJ
63.22    7 |   43    yzAEFGJ
63.21    6 |   33  - yzAEFJ
63.20    6 |   33    yzAEFJ
63.19    4 |   23    yzEF
63.18    4 |   24    yzFJ
63.17    5 |   29    yzEFJ
63.16    5 |   23    yzFJK
63.15    5 |   23    yzFJK
63.14    4 |   23    yFJK
63.13    4     21    yFJK
63.12    4     19    yFJK
63.11    5     18    yEFJK
63.10    5     18    yEFJK
63.09    4      6    yEJK
63.08    2      5    JK
63.07    3      5    yJX
63.06    1      1    y
63.05    1      1    y
63.04    1      1    y
63.03    1      1    y
63.02    1      1    0
```

**12-29 Micro**: Opening sharply higher again, this market receives responsive selling during the initial balance and after. The key question which comes to mind, given the activity of the previous session, is whether or not sellers will continue to respond to the higher prices as expected. Responding as such on the opening, with the opening being only a few ticks off the day's highs, other timeframe sellers continue to create imbalance in the A period, extending the range down 14 ticks and another 18 ticks in B period. Other timeframe buyers, leaving a large buying extreme in B period, push prices back up to the middle of the established range. The market builds value in this area for the remainder of the day.

**12-29 Macro**: Responding to higher prices, the other timeframe sellers are providing another indication that the market may be offering a climaxing top. The absolute top may not yet be in, though, as indicated by the bounce the market exhibits in B period.

TRADING SIMULATOR - Based on the CBOT Market Profile*

DM 0388 13:20:03 63.19  O 63.43  H 63.47  L 62.96  V  776 TB 64^52  TV 371^361
         12/29/87

```
63.47   0    0
63.46   1    2    z
63.45   1    4    z
63.44   1    5    z
63.43   2    9    Oz
63.42   2   12    yz
63.41   2   11    yz
63.40   2   10    yz
63.39   2   10    yz
63.38   2   20    yz
63.37   2   19    yz
63.36   2   11    yz
63.35   2    9    yz
63.34   2   13    yz
63.33   2   14    yz
63.32   1    9    y
63.31   2   10    yA
63.30   2   10    yA
63.29   3   11    yAH
63.28   5   17    yAFGH
63.27   5   24    ADFGH
63.26   6   31    ACDFGH
63.25   6   36    ACDFGH
63.24   5   32    ACDFG
63.23   7   41    ACDFGIJ
63.22   8   44    ACDEFGIJ
63.21   6   41  - ACEFIJ
63.20   8   36    ACDEFIJK
63.19   8   32    ACDEFIJX
63.18   7   32    ACDEIJK
63.17   6   23    ACDIJK
63.16   6   28    ABDIJK
63.15   5   26    ABIJK
63.14   4   13    ABIJ
63.13   2    7    BI
63.12   1    9    B
63.11   1    9    B
63.10   1   10    B
63.09   1   12    B
63.08   1   15    B
63.07   1   14    B
63.06   1   10    B
63.05   1    6    B
63.04   1    2    B
63.03   1    3    B
63.02   1    3    B
63.01   1    2    B
63.00   1    3    B
62.99   1    4    B
62.98   1    9    B
62.97   1   10    B
62.96   1    2    B
```

**12-30 Micro**: This day opens 10 points lower and develops a large initial balance, given the holiday market conditions. Z period forms a buying extreme of 3 ticks. The day then trades within this initial balance. This day is relatively quiet in nature, being the third day which developes value in the same area.

**12-30 Macro**: A consolidation or rest day, and an opportunity for bulls to take profits.

TRADING SIMULATOR - Based on the CBOT Market Profile*

DM 0388 13:20:54 63.16   O 63.10   H 63.27   L 63.02   V   527  TB 46^47   TV 233^227
        12/30/87

```
63.27        0        0
63.26        0        0
63.25        1        1    y
63.24        1        1    F
63.23        2        9    EF
63.22        4       14    yEFG
63.21        4       22    BEFG
63.20        6       31    yBDEFG
63.19        6       23    yBDEFG
63.18        6       33    yBCDEG
63.17        9       36    yBCDEGHIJ
63.16        9       62    yBCEGHIJX
63.15       10       67    yABCEGHIJK
63.14        9       54  - yABCGHIJK
63.13        8       43    yABCHIJK
63.12        6       19    yACHJK
63.11        5       13    yAIJK
63.10        4       14    OzAJ
63.09        4       18    yzAJ
63.08        4       16    yzAJ
63.07        3       11    yzA
63.06        2       12    yz
63.05        2       12    yz
63.04        1        9    z
63.03        1        5    z
63.02        1        1    z
```

**12-31 Micro**: The market opens almost 100 points higher, offering another opportunity to take profits. Y period immediately forms both a selling and a buying extreme, with the selling extreme being more pronounced. A period takes out the selling extreme and C period creates a buying range extension. The day's trade is then confined to the upper half of the day's range.

**12-31 Macro**: The market is culminating or climaxing on a move farther from anything previously seen. Higher prices are advertising for selling, but market-generated information from this time zone's slice of the market does not show that sellers are overwhelming the market, taking profits.

```
TRADING SIMULATOR - Based on the CBOT Market Profile*

DM 0388 12:20:13 64.20  O 64.13  H 64.26  L 63.89  V  741 TB 51^67  TV 243^453
           12/31/87
64.26      0        0
64.25      3       11    CDH
64.24      3       13    CDH
64.23      3       21    CDH
64.22      5       36    CDEHI
64.21      5       37    CDEHI
64.20      5       35    CDEHX
64.19      5       25    CDEHI
64.18      6       28    CDEGHI
64.17      7       35    CDEFGHI
64.16      7       45    CDEFGHI
64.15      7       36    yCDEFGH
64.14      5       23    CDEFG
64.13      5       21    OBDEF
64.12      5       20    yBDEF
64.11      5       13    ABDEF
64.10      4       10    yABF
64.09      3        9    yAB
64.08      3       18    yAB
64.07      3       23  - yAB
64.06      3       22    yAB
64.05      3       25    yAB
64.04      2       13    yA
64.03      3        8    yAB
64.02      2       12    yA
64.01      3       16    yzA
64.00      3       18    yzA
63.99      3       17    yzA
63.98      2       25    yz
63.97      2       40    yz
63.96      2       30    yz
63.95      2       23    yz
63.94      2        8    yz
63.93      2        7    yz
63.92      1        8    y
63.91      1        4    y
63.90      1        3    y
63.89      1        1    y
```

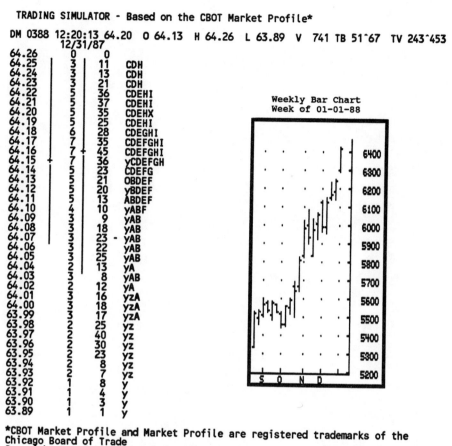

Weekly Bar Chart
Week of 01-01-88

# Chapter 17

# Evolution of the Learning Process

As an individual gains market experience and knowledge, his confidence in his ability to make trading decisions increases. The learning curve, in other words, usually runs parallel to the confidence curve. As successful professionals in other businesses know, the beginning market participant is not inspirited overnight with a transcendental calm and self-assurance. Rather, he feels his ability to confidently make decisions grows gradually, sometimes in barely perceptible stages. With each higher level of confidence comes a corresponding heightened awareness of current market conditions and the growth of a nearly instinctual ability to respond expediently to opportunity and adversity.

### A Map for the Journey: Stage One

The primary significant observation that the trader must make is that price discovery does not occur randomly. It is this fundamental belief that is the basis for any successful trading program. As we have mentioned time and again in these pages, the market, rather than being random, is understandable and can be organized in a format that provides meaning beyond the most recently transacted price. The trader with a modicum of experience watching the markets will come to accept this theoretical basis not as a matter of blind faith but as the operational reality being played out in each trading session. He will see that markets generate information that defines the degree of trade facilitation (the purpose of the market) and the degree of market imbalance (the essence of all directional movement). The market will further display recurrent patterns — each a reflection of the market's response to either balanced or imbalanced situations — and certain corresponding prototypical behaviors.

Happily, the trader's witnessing this logical market behavior serves to comfort him. Aware that the markets have so-called "circuit breakers" — price limits which cause activity to cease — many a novice trader, unschooled in Market Logic, is consumed by the fear that the market can move to a "locked limit" position at any time for days on end. The trader who has observed the markets through the lens of a non-random market model calmly allocates his energy toward other concerns. He knows that such dramatic moves occur under only certain relatively infrequent conditions, most of which can be recognized leading up to the locked-limit session.

A second and no less crucial area of the successful Stage One trader's modus operandi deals with capital and traditional business concerns. A central theme of this book has been that participation in the financial markets is a business like any other business. The logical participant who wishes to be successful structures his program around sound business principles in order to grow over the long term. Yet it is ironic and unfortunate that the financial markets, particularly those which offer a high degree of leverage, attract many with short-term mindsets. The enticing myth of the financial market depicts the trading floor as a place where a little money and some luck can be spun overnight into a fortune. The successful trader's program treats this mindset as anathema from the very start. The individual who positions heavily on a single situation is bound to fail. The individual who structures his trading program to win over a large sample size, on the other hand, has a chance to succeed.

Once accepting long-term objectives as a logical imperative, most traders still lack an overall money management game plan that affords them staying power during the learning curve. Their neglect of capital concerns frequently accounts for emotional trading decisions which are based on information having nothing to do with actual market behavior. Most market participants are conditioned to think that when using leverage they should be prepared to lose some or all of the funds placed in their accounts. A successful capital management and trading structure completely opposes this defeatist expectation. The premise on which a sound trading/investing philosophy is based is simply this: "Don't lose principal." Under this regimen capital preservation is the primary goal of the program.

Of course, the degree to which capital preservation is valued ahead of seeking to make profits can be placed on a spectrum of trading styles, from conservative to aggressive. When results are favorable, both the aggressive and conservative trading styles profit, with the aggressive style generating higher returns. However, when trading results are mixed, the aggressive account suffers sizable drawdowns while the conservative account merely falls back on the cushion of profits it has accrued. Since

losses are an inevitable part of trading, it follows
that over a large sample size, a conservative
approach offers a greater probability of sustained
success and limited exposure, by increasing the
duration of staying power when one is "out of
step" with the markets.

Certainly, trading an aggressive approach,
provided all factors fall into place, will generate
greater profits than a conservative approach.
However, a risk management policy that starts
with conservative trades and moves to an
aggressive posture as results allow also has the
potential to provide sizable rewards. This concept
can best be likened to the strategy of a football
team which takes an early lead during the game.
With a few points on the scoreboard to cushion
against error, the team is able to comfortably
initiate riskier plays in an effort to score greater
results.

Risk      management      through      volatility
assessment/diversification is another central
element of a logical capital management plan.
Critical to the formation of such a program is the
control of risk through proper allocation of trading
funds. Simply put, results will be influenced in
large part by how volatile the market is and how
much volatility one is exposed to as a function of
the level of funding available.

### Negotiating the Terrain: Stage Two

When a trader reaches the second stage of
market understanding, he has achieved a working
familarity with market-generated information on
a short timeframe basis and is ready to exploit this
knowledge for longer term goals. Knowing that
markets are not random and that they at times
trend, the trader concentrates on positioning
himself in the direction of the trend that offers the
greatest opportunity. The seasoned trader,

comfortable now in using day structure information to his advantage, can devote more energy to seeking out longer term trends. He knows that despite the dynamic nature of the markets, he can only hope to succeed in a limited number of major moves in a given year. Nonetheless, his new primary ambition should be to lengthen his timeframe and to feel comfortable holding profitable trades as long as possible.

He further becomes adept at detecting and evaluating the "micro" information that is the basis for identifying big markets early. He sees, for instance, that the market moves in daily, weekly and longer term cycles — continually vacillating from quiet to volatile, bull to bear, and sideways to trending market conditions — and displays numerous recurring patterns along the way. For example, bull markets tend to open lower and close higher more often than not. They tend to have daily lows occur within the first hour — within the first thirty minutes more often than not. They tend to close strongly on the week and month, settling on or near the highs at the week's or month's end. The seasoned trader has seen for himself that certain day structures — a trend day up, a normal variation day up — tend to be formed more frequently in bull moves than in sideways markets. And most importantly, the Stage Two trader detects imbalance in the market, frequently by simply noting this on his Long Term Market Activity Chart.

The trader now has an arsenal of analytical tools as he sets out beyond the scope of the day with which to identify and take advantage of the trend. Market-generated information is used within a larger context to avoid overemphasizing the day's activity at the expense of missing the broad move. The trader has arrived at the stage where, rather than wasting energy inspecting each and every piece of foliage, he sees the proverbial forest for the trees.

The Stage Two trader now strives for a consistent decision-making routine which best balances his comfort level, aggressiveness, and ability to read market-generated information. The goal is to systematically categorize each market into one of several types of prototypical market conditions, determining if he is "in step" with longer term market behavior. It is through this organized approach that exacting trade location can be enhanced and sound "trade management" practices can be maintained.

Trade management refers to the daily assessment of open or possible market positions in terms of an overall bias toward the trade. Proper trade management dictates that market conditions and possible scenarios should be evaluated in each trade before the market opening. In determining a bias toward each trade for the day, trades can be categorized into one of three groups: 1) problem trades, 2) trades that pose a concern, and 3) trades that are unfolding according to plan. As the day develops, the challenge is to monitor the markets, looking for signs which would a) lead to exiting problem trades, b) shift trades from category to category as is warranted, and c) enter new trades (or add to existing okay trades) when good trade location can be had. When the market is unfolding as expected, the degree of scrutiny with which the trade is managed may be lessened so as not to distract the trader from other opportunities.

### Over the Top: Stage Three

A trader in the third stage of market awareness assumes a mastery of the mechanical methodology introduced in this book. The master is able to extract these operational strategies and apply them in an unself-conscious manner in his trading. Decision-making in the financial markets once mastery is attained, requires as much thought as writing one's signature. Not that attaining the level of confidence herein labeled mastery means that each and every trade is a dramatic home run. But experience and resulting confidence allow the master to focus energy on being the best he can be.

Indeed, a level of decision-making mastery cannot be attained until one has met with some significant level of failure. Having met with enough of it, having dealt with it, and having resolved to adjust so as to avoid it, the decision-maker loses a subconscious fear of failure. Not afraid of the numerous outcomes of any given situation, the master knows he has handled and will again be able to handle whatever adverse behavior the market exhibits. Unfettered, he maintains an open-mindedness, confidently and consistently arriving at decisions without over-intellectualizing the decision-making process.

We have examined tools which organize transactional data and support a decision-making process approach. While this work has focused on analysis of market-generated information, we in no way advocate discarding fundamental analysis. There are two simple ways to ascertain value: through fundamental analysis and through the analysis of market-generated information. Both support each other and are therefore valuable support tools for all participants. Rather than being gleaned from an accounting analysis, market-generated information is garnered directly from the market and is therefore more current. However, just like a conclusion based on last month's balance sheet, a conclusion reached from an interpretation of market-generated information is also temporary, since in all aspects of reality, conditions change. In other words, just as the portfolio manager must study each new balance sheet so as to monitor whether earnings continue to remain strong while liabilities are steady or shrinking, so must today's active manager monitor market-generated information, deciding whether the selling imbalance subsides and strong buying activity arises. Conditions change, and the successful manager updates his conclusions based on the most recent information available. All professionals in financial markets must manage and remain flexible to changing information. Keep in mind that while there are tremendous advantages to adding an analysis of market-generated information to a decision-making process, its addition will be no mystical panacea, despite what others may have you believe.

The level of attainment we label as the master decision-maker in the financial markets will unfortunately continue to be misunderstood. To begin with, in any area of human endeavor a small percentage of the participating population will excel, often causing envy and jealousy, not necessarily among those less successfully engaged in the pursuit, but in those who choose not to pursue. While everyone cannot attain the highest level of outward success, the master realizes that his goals should not be outwardly motivated; indeed, his attaining them need not serve notice to anyone else. He is difficult for society to categorize and classify. A professional in all meanings of the word, he is a specialist trained in the behavior of markets under varying conditions, who is able to make conclusions based on data that do not make sense to one who does not have the background and understanding that is earned through formal training and years of experience. And yet, the trading decision-maker must also be considered a businessman, since he applies the sound rules of logic and deductive reasoning to the challenge of managing money in an eternally changing environment. He does not ask to be paid for his failures, and competes with no one other than himself. Indeed, he admires success and achievement by others.

He embraces the ideal that his net worth is his ability to function. He maintains faith in himself and his ability to handle all situations. He disciplines himself to do what is right once he has decided to do it. And he does not confuse his self-worth with his most recent success or failure.